THE LUNE VALLEY
AND THE HOWGILLS

A WALKING GUIDE

About the Authors

Both native Lancastrians, Dennis and Jan Kelsall have long held a passion for countryside and hill walking. Since their first Cicerone title was published in 1995, they have written and illustrated around 35 guides covering some of Britain's most popular walking areas and regularly contribute to various outdoor magazines. Their enjoyment of the countryside extends far beyond a love of fresh air, the freedom of open spaces and an appreciation of scenery. Over the years Dennis and Jan have developed a wider interest in the environment, its geology and wildlife, as well as an enthusiasm for delving into the local history that so often provides clues to interpreting the landscape.

Other Cicerone guides by the authors
The Pembrokeshire Coastal Path
The Ribble Way
The Yorkshire Dales: North and East
The Yorkshire Dales: South and West
Walking in Pembrokeshire

THE LUNE VALLEY AND THE HOWGILLS

A WALKING GUIDE

by Dennis and Jan Kelsall

2 POLICE SQUARE, MILNTHORPE, CUMBRIA LA7 7PY
www.cicerone.co.uk

© Dennis and Jan Kelsall 2012
First edition 2012
ISBN: 978 1 85284 668 8

Printed by KHL Printing, Singapore

A catalogue record for this book is available from the British Library.
All photographs are by the author unless otherwise stated.

This product includes mapping data licensed from Ordnance Survey® with the permission of the Controller of Her Majesty's Stationery Office. © Crown copyright 2012. All rights reserved. Licence number PU100012932.

Front cover: Across the Lune Valley to the Howgills from Firbank

CONTENTS

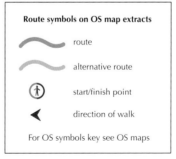

Route symbols on OS map extracts

route

alternative route

start/finish point

direction of walk

For OS symbols key see OS maps

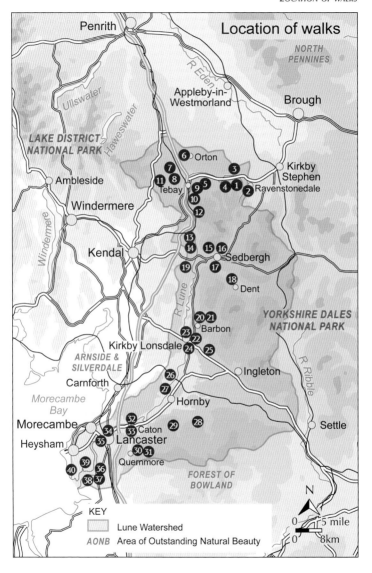

Location of walks

Penrith

R Eden

NORTH
PENNINES

Appleby-in-
Westmorland

Brough

Ullswater

Haweswater

LAKE DISTRICT
NATIONAL PARK

6 Orton

3

7

11
8
Tebay
9 5
10
4 1
2

Kirkby
Stephen
Ravenstonedale

Ambleside

Windermere

12

Windermere

13
14
15 16
Sedbergh
17

Kendal

19

18
Dent

R Lune

YORKSHIRE DALES
NATIONAL PARK

20 21
Barbon
23
22
24
25

R Ribble

ARNSIDE &
SILVERDALE

Kirkby Lonsdale

Ingleton

Carnforth

26
27
Hornby

Morecambe
Bay

32
33 Caton
29

28

Settle

Morecambe

34

Lancaster

Heysham

35

39
36
40
38 37

30 31
Quernmore

FOREST OF
BOWLAND

N

KEY

Lune Watershed

AONB Area of Outstanding Natural Beauty

0   5 mile
0   8km

7

Through a gap in the wall along Borrowdale towards Blease Fell (Walk 11)

INTRODUCTION

The area of the Lune valley, nestled between the Lake District and the Yorkshire Dales, begs discovery and presents no shortage of inviting walks to suit every taste and inclination. The selection of walks in this guide reveals its many facets, with routes that clamber onto the hills overlooking the main valley, delve into the tributary dales that feed it, or simply follow the River Lune itself. Further downstream the routes wander the two promontories between which the Lune finally meets the sea near Lancaster, seeking out the many picturesque and interesting corners there. In some walks, aspects of the area's rich history are revealed, while few rambles lack opportunities to observe wildlife at any time of year. Walking is one of the best forms of physical exercise, and in a setting such as this, it cannot help but be good for the mind and soul too.

Although it gives its name to Lancashire, the River Lune is born in what was Westmorland, a historic county that was swallowed up within Cumbria during the reorganisation of local government in 1974. The river's higher reaches fall from the Howgill Fells in a fold that separates the western dales of Yorkshire from the rolling hills of south-east Lakeland. The river enters Lancashire only below Kirkby Lonsdale, but immediately encounters

Looking back past the Lune Viaduct towards Arant Haw (Walk 14)

9

Beached boats indicate that the high tide covers the salt marsh (Walk 40)

some of the county's prettiest country-side. Lower down it skirts the Forest of Bowland before passing through Lancaster to find eventual release into Morecambe Bay and the Irish Sea.

Although surrounded by hills, it is the Howgill Fells to which the Lune is most intimately related, that distinctive massif of high ground rising dramatically to the east of the M6 as it passes through the deep trough of the Lune Gorge. The tentacles of the river's upper tributaries completely encircle this compact group and effectively set it apart from the neighbouring Pennine and Lakeland hills.

The Lune is a relatively short river, yet it embraces a considerable upland sweep that includes The Calf and all the other high tops of the Howgills, a corner of the Shap Fells, as well as the southern aspect of Great Asby Scar. Further south, Whernside and most of Ingleborough also lie within its reach, the catchment curving around to include the northern slopes of the Forest of Bowland. But the area explored within this book is not confined to the high hills, and there is much of interest too within the main valley and its tributaries. Borrowdale, Dentdale and the secluded valleys of Bowland are particularly beautiful, while the estuarine marshes and coast reveal other aspects of the area's character.

Besides Lancaster, Kirkby Lonsdale and Sedbergh are the only towns situated by the river, and the area is largely untouched by conurbation or industry. The beckoning landscape ranges from the untamed, expansive moorlands of the high tops to secluded woods, bucolic countryside and tide-washed coast, all combining to offer walking that is both varied and rewarding. Although there are undoubtedly challenges to be found, none of the routes included here is overly demanding. They focus upon walking for enjoyment to appreciate the scenery, wildlife and plants encountered while the text also offers background to some of the features and curiosities passed along the way.

Traditionally, the river is regarded as upwelling from the ground beside the mound of an ancient chapel dedicated to St Helen in the hamlet of Newbiggin-on-Lune, although higher and longer tributaries complicate any discussion of its source. The river's 50-odd mile journey to the coast winds almost entirely through unspoiled countryside, and along its length the river subtly exchanges the wild scenery of rolling, deserted moorland hills for a more intimate pastoral setting of waterside meadows and woodland.

Scattered throughout the upper Lune Valley are attractive farmsteads, hamlets and villages, with only two settlements large enough to claim the status of town, Kirkby Lonsdale and Sedbergh (the latter being set back a couple of miles from the main flow). Both ancient market centres, they retain a delightful individuality that is becoming increasingly hard to find in today's towns. They make ideal bases for a few days' exploration of the area or convenient stopping-off points for those wishing to create an 'end-to-end' trek along the valley.

Looking back to Beckside from the path to Harprigg (Walk 19)

The only major conurbation within the river's entire catchment is Lancaster, founded by the Romans as a garrisoned port at the river's lowest bridging point. Throughout the Middle Ages the County Palatine of Lancaster was governed from its intimidating medieval castle and, although the county's administrative centre has now shifted south to Preston, Lancaster is still considered the county town. During the 18th century it rivalled Liverpool as a great seaport, trading with the Baltic States, Africa and the Americas, but with a silting estuary and shifting centres of economic activity, Lancaster's maritime importance faded into history. Downstream, the city is quickly left behind and the river, tidal from this point, winds to a lonely estuary across an expanse of largely empty coastal plain, where extensive salt marsh and mud flats attract a host of birds to feed at low water.

The landscape through which the river flows boasts great beauty and diversity, yet much of the main valley, let alone its many tributary dales, is relatively unknown and little visited, overshadowed by the proximity of more well-publicised neighbours. Few of those passing through to the Lake District, the Yorkshire Dales or points further north afford it little more than a passing glance and most are largely oblivious to the loveliness of its uncluttered countryside. The Howgill Fells and the Forest of Bowland are among the country's least frequented hills, and few but locals are aware of the attractive hamlets and villages scattered along the length of the valley.

Across the Lune Valley from the top of Firbank (Walk 14)

The rewards of such relative obscurity are found in unfrequented hills and vales, an absence of the trappings of commercialism, and a freedom from the obligation to undertake a handful of 'must do' routes. In and around the Lune there are no 'highest peaks' to climb or 'longest ridges' to traverse, and the one or two spots that have gained a justified popularity have yet to succumb to over-exploitation. Travelling from one end of the valley to the other reveals an ever-changing scene that is constantly and subtly altering to offer something uniquely special.

Much of the upland catchment is open-access land where walkers can roam at will, while miles of paths, trackways and quiet lanes offer endless scope for inquisitive and uncrowded explorations. The revelation of far-reaching views from the tops contrasts with the intimacy of secluded woodlands and deep, winding valleys, while the abundance of plant and wildlife and endless wayside curiosities more than matches that to be found along the well-worn trails of the more popular haunts.

ORIGINS AND LANDSCAPE

The waters of the Lune
Identifying the origin of any river depends upon the rules by which you want to play – highest point, longest course, farthest from the sea and so on. An unambiguous answer is rare, and the River Lune is no exception.

The first reference to its name on the map is the hamlet of Newbiggin-on-Lune, where the river is held to bubble up from the ancient and holy perennial spring of St Helen's Well. Other authorities point out that the stream below the village is called Sandwath Beck, and only beyond its confluence with Weasdale Beck, a mile downstream at Wath, does it become the Lune. Yet by the time its reaches Newbiggin, Sandwath Beck is already into its third name, having started life out as Dale Gill and then become Greenside Beck. Up the hill behind Newbiggin, Dale Gill issues from a couple of uncertain springs, just below the summit of Green Bell, and it is from here that longest meandering course to the sea can be traced.

However, the consideration of height adds yet another factor to the debate. Without doubt, at 723m Ingleborough is the river's most lofty source, although any rain falling on the summit is immediately sucked into the labyrinth of fissures, pots and caves beneath the mountain and only reappears much lower down its flanks. The beginning of the highest continuous stream is a shallow tarn at around 665m on the summit of Baugh Fell, from which flows the River Rawthey. Perhaps the only way to be certain of having dipped your toe in the river's source is to visit all five locations.

13

Built in the 18th century, Smardale Bridge straddles Scandal Beck (Walk 2)

Whatever its beginnings, the River Lune has a catchment extending over 430 square miles (1114km²), but it is peculiarly one-sided in that, for much of its length, the western watershed is less than two miles from the river, so all major input is from the east. The only significant streams that contradict this lopsidedness are Birk Beck and Borrowdale, which fall from the Shap Fells on the fringe of the Lake District National Park, and Chapel Beck and Raise Beck, springs seeping from the limestone of Great Asby Scar, which overlooks the budding river from the north. The Lune's infant tendrils almost completely encircle the Howgill massif, with only a couple of streams that feed Scandal Beck escaping capture to flow northwards into the River Eden. Further south the Lune's tributaries penetrate deep into the western dales of North Yorkshire, stealing all the rills and rivulets from Baugh Fell, Whernside and the majority of those from Ingleborough too. Even in its final stages, the Lune maintains its intimacy with the high hills, for the northern slopes of the Bowland fells also come within its grasp.

Landscape

While the Lune catchment lacks the unified identity that designation as a national park or AONB creates, it impinges upon the existing national parks of the Lake District and Yorkshire Dales, as well as the Forest of Bowland Area of Outstanding Natural Beauty. Proposed national park boundary changes would extend this by bringing virtually all the catchment north of

Kirkby Lonsdale within one or other of the existing national parks and would be a formal recognition of its special qualities. The catchment compares well with both the scale and character of such designated areas in Britain, for although only half the size of the Lake District, it is double that of the New Forest. The sheer variety of its unblemished landscape is compelling, and ranges from remote upland fell, crag and rambling moor through ancient woodland and rolling pasture to tidal marsh and coast. Threading through it all is the Lune itself, a river of ever-changing mood sustained by countless springs, becks, streams and lesser rivers, which each display a different facet of the valley's beguiling character.

Although surrounded by mountainous ground, the abrupt mass of the **Howgill Fells** stands apart and is obviously different from all around. Severed from the volcanic rocks of the Lakeland hills by the Lune Gorge, and from the Dales limestone by the Dent Fault, the daunting flanks guard a citadel of high plateau grounded on ancient shales and sandstones, which is deeply incised by steep-sided, narrow valleys that penetrate its heart. Any approach from the south demands a stiff climb to gain the broad, grassy ridges that radiate from its high point, **The Calf**, but if you settle for a longer walk the more gently inclined fingers that extend to the north offer something less energetic but equally rewarding. The tops have been rounded smooth by erosion over countless millennia to leave few crags or rocky faces; however, where

A moment's pause to enjoy the view along Bowderdale (Walk 4)

they occur, they can be dramatic and create impressive waterfalls. Unlike the neighbouring hills, the fells have never been fenced or walled, and grazing sheep and wild ponies wander unimpeded across the slopes. The walker, too, can range at will and experience a wonderful sense of remoteness, although a paucity of definite landmarks and the confusing geography of the ridges can make navigation something of a challenge when the cloud is down.

Flanking the infant Lune to the north are the more gently rising slopes of **Great Asby Scar**, which is protected as a National Nature Reserve for its expanse of limestone pavement. Scoured of their overburden by the moving ice sheet, and subsequently littered with erratic boulders as the ice

retreated at the end of the last ice age, the bare limestone beds are crazed by grikes (fissures created as the slight acidity of rainwater exploits natural cracks and crevices). The deep fissures separating the clints (blocks) collect windblown soil and moisture, and harbour a surprising range of plants and even occasional trees that would otherwise be unable to survive these desert-like conditions.

Collecting the waters flowing from the peaty mosses flanking the Shap Fells, the river turns abruptly south at Tebay to enter the **Lune Gorge**. Squeezed between steeply rising hills, the valley follows the line of a geological fault, which was further deepened by ice moving from the north. It is perhaps the Lune's most dramatic section, and, despite the

Looking back to Grayrigg Common and Tebay Fell (Walk 13)

fact that both railway and motorway have been shoehorned in alongside the original road, the river retains a delightful separateness and one can meander through, oblivious of the intrusion. The heights on either side offer superb views across the valley, and the twisting gorge of **Carlin Gill** is one of the Howgills' particular gems. Entering from the west, **Borrowdale** is another little-known delight. Simply wandering along the base of the secluded valley is enjoyment in itself, but include the traverse across **Whinfell Common** and the day could not be more complete.

Motorway and inter-city rail break out of the valley at Lowgill, leaving the river to a gently wooded passage below the lesser hills of **Firbank Fell**. As the gorge then opens out beyond the Howgills, the River Rawthey joins the flow, bringing with it the River Dee from Dentdale and Clough River out of Garsdale. The hills now take a step back, allowing the river to snake across a broad floodplain that extends all the way south until the valley of the Lune is abruptly constricted once more at Kirkby Lonsdale. The heights of **Middleton Fell** are a fine vantage, revealing a dramatic glimpse into Barbondale and across to Crag Hill and Whernside, while the dales converging on **Sedbergh** and the lower hills around **Killington** offer alternative perspectives on the river's middle course.

Below **Kirkby Lonsdale** the valley opens wide again, and the bluffs

on the western bank – although lower than the hills rising to the east – tend to nudge the river on its way. Things were not always so, for the Lune's course over time has been erratic, and old banks, stranded pools and dry channels betray where it once flowed. Rivers from the limestone heart of the Yorkshire Dales enter from the east, where the flat-topped summit of Ingleborough erupts as a dominant landmark. The karst landscape of the area is noted as much for what lies below the surface as above, and an amble into the valley of **Leck Beck** reveals some of the portals to this hidden world. Further south lie the **Bowland fells**, another neglected moorland upland where walkers can experience unfettered wandering and expansive panoramas, a contrast to the tracts of ancient woodland to be found in the deep vales that drain it.

Approaching **Lancaster**, the River Lune becomes tidal and enters its final phase. At the city's maritime height, the riverbanks were hives of activity, lined with mills, shipyards, quays and warehouses. Some of the old buildings remain, having found new life as residential accommodation, but elsewhere today's commercial enterprise no longer depends upon the river and instead faces towards the streets and roads. The riverbank now forms part of a Millennium Park that follows the Lune from Caton to **Glasson**, a pleasant, traffic-free conduit for walkers and cyclists to and from the heart of the city along the line of a former

Beyond Springs Wood, the path briefly closes with Leck Beck (Walk 25)

railway. Its centrepiece is a striking modern bridge spanning the river at Lancaster that brings in another trail from the coast at Morecambe.

Skirting a belt of low drumlins, formed from till deposited along the coastal fringe of glaciation, the Lune winds on to its **estuary**, where it finally breaks free of the land. Enclosure and drainage during the 19th century have reclaimed some of the low-lying moss (coastal marsh) as farmland, but beyond the flood dikes there remains a vast area of tide-washed mud, sandbanks and grazing salt marsh. The **Plover Scar Light** marks the obvious end of the river, but its channel is mapped between the sands for a further 4 miles (6.4km) to the Point of Lune, where it finally loses its identity within Morecambe Bay.

HISTORY

Man's impact on the Lune catchment and corridor has been, in many ways, less intrusive than it has on many of Britain's other rivers. Nevertheless, it remains very much a man-made landscape. Climate change and prehistoric clearance of the upland forests for farming have created the open moorland we value today, and the network of field and pasture along the valleys is the product of generations of agricultural management.

Although meagre, visible evidence of man's ancient presence can be found upon the landscape. While not rivalling the scale of Stonehenge, there are stone circles on the flank of Orton Fell and above Casterton, and there are several known settlement sites, including an area above Cowan

Bridge and, of course, the massive fort on top of Ingleborough.

The Romans used the trough of the Lune as a route north from forts at Lancaster and Ribchester. Their road followed the valley all the way to Tebay before climbing over Crosby Ravensworth Fell, and there were camps beside the River Lune opposite Whittington and at the foot of Borrowdale.

Later, the valley fell under the authority of Tostig, Earl of Northumberland and brother of Harold Godwinson, the last Anglo-Saxon king of England. Tostig's ambitions for the throne ended with his death at the Battle of Stamford Bridge in September 1066, but Harold's victory was short-lived, for within the month William, Duke of Normandy landed at Pevensey, and on 14 October defeated Harold at Hastings.

The Normans quickly established their authority in the southern part of England, but the north was a different matter. The Lune Valley became seen as a strategic frontier passage, and for a time, the Welsh Marches apart, it was one of the most heavily fortified areas in the country, with some ten motte and bailey castles being built in and around the valley between Tebay and Lancaster.

But normality slowly returned, and the Norman age saw the founding of many religious communities up and down the country, with isolated riverside settings often chosen as the site of an abbey. Much of the upper Lune was incorporated within the estates of monasteries as far away as Byland in Yorkshire, yet only three houses were established within the valley itself. The ruins of a small Gilbertine priory can be

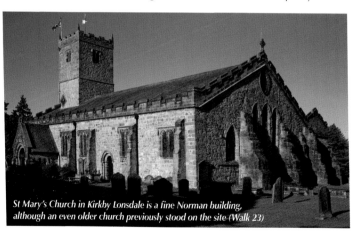

St Mary's Church in Kirkby Lonsdale is a fine Norman building, although an even older church previously stood on the site (Walk 23)

Completed in 1860, the Lune Viaduct carried the railway between Ingleton and Lowgill (Walk 14)

seen at Ravenstonedale, while St Mary's at Lancaster is a priory church founded under the Benedictines. The third monastery was on the coast at Cockersand, established by the Premonstratensian order.

The only significant settlement along the river's course, Lancaster developed as a port and centre of manufacture, but the power of the river and its side-streams was never exploited on an industrial scale in the way of other Lancashire and Yorkshire rivers. As the river was not navigable above Lancaster, the hinterland was left relatively remote from other areas, and any small centres served largely local needs. Thus, when the canal age arrived, there was no industry to justify investment in extending the Lancaster Canal into the Lune Valley. The railway engineers, like the

Romans, saw it purely as a convenient route to the north, although Tebay and Barbon saw a brief expansion with the line's arrival, and the brick industry at Claughton benefited from its passing.

Today's travellers often pass through the area on the way to the better-known attractions of the Lake District and the Yorkshire Dales, and earlier travellers were no different. William Gilpin had his sights set upon the lands beyond the 'bay of Cartmel', and passed through Lancaster on his way to Kendal. The castle failed to impress, 'an indifferent object from any point', but the Lune he regarded as a 'notable piece of water, [which] when the tide is full, sufficiently adorns the landscape'.

In 1772 Lancaster's quay was busy with ships, and Gilpin ventured a little way upriver to describe its passage through Lonsdale. His words might very well apply today, 'where quietly, and unobserved, it winds around projecting rocks – forms circling boundaries to meadows, pastured with cattle – and passes through groves and thickets, which in fabulous times, might have been the haunt of wood-gods. In one part, taking a sudden turn, it circles a little, delicious spot, forming into a peninsula called vulgarly, "the wheel of Lune".'

Three years earlier while on his way to Settle, Thomas Gray had gazed up the valley towards Ingleborough and been moved to pen 'every feature which constitutes a perfect landscape of the extensive sort is here not only boldly marked, but in its best position'. JMW Turner stayed a little longer to capture the scene at the Crook o'Lune and painted a landscape from beside the church at Kirkby Lonsdale. The picture so impressed Ruskin that he took the trouble to go and see for himself and the spot became known as 'Ruskin's View' and not Turner's.

WILDLIFE

With little habitation and no industry along its course, the River Lune is one of England's cleanest rivers and consequently rich in wildlife. It is one of the most important salmon rivers in the country, and the fish returning upriver from the Atlantic to breed can sometimes be seen leaping from the water. Sea and river trout are also among the fish frequenting the river.

Once abundant, too, were eels that breed in the Sargasso Sea but grow and mature in the estuaries and rivers of western Europe. Rare, but still present, are colonies of white crayfish and pearl mussels, and conservation projects are being undertaken to improve their habitats.

Otters might be spotted, and there are known to be several holts from Halton all the way up to Tebay, although the Crook o'Lune is a good place to watch for them. Badger, roe deer, fox and hare all roam the surrounding countryside as, of course, do rabbit and grey squirrel. Britain's native red squirrel, however, is now rare, but remains precariously established at the top end of the river around Newbiggin.

Above all, birds can be seen wherever you go, and a field guide is an indispensable companion. Beside the river, heron, oystercatcher, sandmartin, goosandar and ducks are all common,

A hare in Bretherdale (Walk 8)

21

Even at the edge of Lancaster, there is plenty of bird life to be seen by the river (Walk 35)

remains rich in wildflowers. Oak, ash, hazel, alder, holly and hawthorn provide cover for a wide range of flowers, with carpets of snowdrops, ransoms and bluebells as well as many other species being commonly found. Flowers are at their best in spring and early summer, but late summer is the time to appreciate the full glory of the moors, when the heather is in flower. Autumn brings the rich colour of turning leaves, but is also the time when the mysterious world of fungi comes into its own.

TRANSPORT

All sections of the Lune Valley are readily accessible from the M6 motorway, and Lancaster, Oxenholme (on the eastern fringe of Kendal) and Penrith stations are all on the West Coast mainline.

Local bus services visit some villages, but rural timetables are not always geared to the needs of walkers, and it is as well to check details in advance (www.traveline.org.uk).

If you travel by car, be aware that the lanes of the area are generally narrow, winding and occasionally steep and were never intended for today's traffic. Extra care is needed as slow-moving farm vehicles, animals, pedestrians, horse riders and cyclists may lie around any corner. Wherever possible use official car parks, but if none is available, park considerately and ensure that you do not obstruct field or farm access or cause damage to the verge.

but keep a look out as well for the kingfisher. Wander into the wooded tributary valleys to find warblers, flycatchers and woodpeckers, with dippers and wagtails flitting around the streams. Barn owls, too, roam the area, their main food being small mammals such as voles. The moors are important nesting sites for lapwing, curlew and golden plover, and upon the Bowland hills can be found the merlin, Britain's smallest falcon, and the hen harrier, which the AONB has adopted for its logo. Many species come to the estuary to feed and, dependent upon the tide, you may well see flocks of waders, geese and swans.

Grazing and agriculture have displaced the flower meadows that would once have spilled across the valley, but hedgerows and an abundance of small natural woodlands in the many deep side-branches mean that the area

Farmers have their ways and means of herding sheep – you never know what might be round the next bend in the road (Walk 19)

ACCOMMODATION AND FACILITIES

Hotels, bed and breakfast and self-catering cottages are widely available at the main centres of Lancaster, Kirkby Lonsdale and Sedbergh, as well as in many of the villages. There is also a good selection of camping and caravan sites. (For websites giving accommodation details, see Appendix C.) The many local pubs, restaurants and cafés offer appetising menus, often based around locally produced foods and specialities. There are banks and post offices at the main centres, but several hamlets have regrettably lost all their services, including the local shop and pub. As elsewhere in the country, mobile phone coverage is biased towards centres of population, and in the hill areas reception can be patchy.

NAVIGATION AND MAPS

The mapping extracts (1:50,000) accompanying each walk in this guide indicate the outline of the route and are not intended as a substitute for taking the map itself with you. The context of the wider area given by the larger scale (1:25,000) OS Explorer maps will not only add to the enjoyment of identifying neighbouring hills and other features, but is vital should you wander off course or need to find an alternative way back. Reference to the route description and appropriate map will avoid most navigational difficulties, but on upland routes competence in the use of a compass is necessary, particularly if there is a risk of poor visibility.

A GPS receiver (and spare batteries) can be a useful additional aid, but you should know how to use it

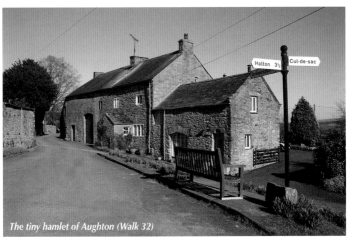

The tiny hamlet of Aughton (Walk 32)

A view across the foot of Lunesdale from a splendid stone stile (Walk 5)

and be conscious of its shortcomings. Be aware of your own limitations and do not start out if anticipated conditions are likely to be beyond your experience. If the weather unexpectedly deteriorates, always be prepared to turn back.

The area is covered by Ordnance Survey maps at both 1:25,000 and 1:50,000 scales, but the larger scale shows a greater detail that is often invaluable.

The Ordnance Survey Explorer maps for the walks in this guide are listed below.

- OL19 (Howgill Fells and Upper Eden Valley)
- OL7 (The English Lakes, South Eastern area)
- OL2 (Yorkshire Dales, Southern and Western areas)
- OL41 (Forest of Bowland and Ribblesdale)
- 296 (Lancaster, Morecambe and Fleetwood)

PLANNING YOUR WALK

Safety

None of the routes described in this book is technically demanding, but be aware that after very heavy rain rivers and streams can flood, rendering paths beside them temporarily impassable. A handful of walks venture onto upland moors, where paths may be vague or non-existent and conditions can be very different from those experienced in the valley. The weather can rapidly deteriorate at any time of year and inexperienced walkers should be aware that it is easy to become disorientated in mist.

Walking with a companion can add to the enjoyment of the day and provide an element of safety. If you venture out alone, it is a good idea to notify someone of your intended route and return time, rather than leave a note on the dashboard of your car as an open invitation to a thief.

Following the simple and common-sense advice below will help ensure that you get the best out of the day.

Timings

Plan your walk in advance, bearing in mind your own and your companions' capabilities and the anticipated weather conditions for the day. The times given in the box at the start of each walk are based on distance (2½ miles per hour) and height gain (1 minute per 10m of ascent), but make no allowance for rest or photographic stops along the way. They are provided merely as a guide, and in practice your own time may significantly differ, depending upon your level of fitness, ability to cope with the terrain and other factors such as weather.

Gradient, poor conditions underfoot and lousy weather can add considerably to both time and effort. If you are new to walking, begin with some of the shorter or less demanding walks to gain a measure of your performance.

Footpaths and tracks

The network of public footpaths and tracks in the area is extensive, and signposts and waymarks are generally well positioned to confirm the route. On the upper moors, and indeed across many of the valley meadows, the actual line of the path is not always distinct, but the way is often discernible along a 'trod'. Defined as a 'mark made by treading', a trod, by its nature,

Heading towards Arant Haw in the Howgills under glowering skies (Walk 15)

becomes increasingly obvious the more it is walked, and indeed may develop over time as a path. But on the upper slopes it is a less tangible thing – a slight flattening of the grass punctuated by an occasional boot print. A trod may differ from a sheep track only in that it has purposeful direction, and an element of concentration is often required to stay on the right course.

Clothing and footwear

Wear appropriate clothing and footwear and carry a comfortable rucksack. The variability of British weather can pack all four seasons into a single day – sun, rain, wind and snow, with the temperature bobbing up and down like a yo-yo. All this makes deciding what to wear potentially difficult, but the best advice is to be prepared for everything, and with today's technical fabrics this is not as hard as it may seem.

Lightweight jackets and trousers can be both windproof and waterproof, without being too cumbersome should the weather improve. Efficient underlayers of manmade fabric wick away the damp to keep you warm and dry, and throwing in an extra fleece takes up little extra room. Good quality socks will help keep feet comfortable and warm, and don't forget gloves and a hat. In summer, a sun hat and lotion offer protection against UV, and shorts aren't always a good idea, particularly where there are nettles and brambles.

Whether you choose leather or fabric boots is a matter of personal preference, but ensure that they are waterproof rather than merely water-resistant. Boots should, of course, be comfortable and offer both good ankle support and grip.

Food and drink

A number of walks pass a pub or a café at some stage, but if you are intending to rely on them check in advance that they will be open. Even so, it is always a good idea to carry extra 'emergency rations' in case of the unforeseen. Ensure, too, that you carry plenty to drink, particularly when the weather is warmer, as dehydration can be a significant problem.

USING THIS GUIDE

This collection of walks includes something for everyone, from novices to experienced ramblers, and the routes range in distance from 3 to 11 miles (4.8 to 22.5km). While the lengthier walks require an appropriate degree of physical fitness, none demands scrambling or climbing ability. The area is hilly rather than mountainous, and gradients are generally moderate, with any steep sections usually brief.

All the walks are either circular or there-and-back walks, and so return to the starting point. They are arranged geographically in the guide, starting with the walks in the north of the region and gradually following the river southwards to the sea.

Each route description begins with a box that provides essential information about the walk, including the distance and time, as well as details of useful facilities such as refreshments, toilets and parking. In the route description, key navigational places and features are shown in **bold**.

Three appendixes provide a route summary table (Appendix A), a description of a longer route from one end of the Lune Valley to the other (Appendix B), and a list of contact details (Appendix C).

Enjoying a walk beside the Lancaster Canal (Walk 37)

WALK 1
Weasdale and Randygill Top

Start Point	Wath (NY 685 050)
Distance	8 miles (12.9km)
Time	4¼hrs
Terrain	Rough tracks and upland trods
Height Gain	560m (1837ft)
Maps	Explorer OL19 – Howgill Fells and Upper Eden Valley
Refreshments	Lune Spring Garden Centre café at Newbiggin-on-Lune
Toilets	None
Parking	Roadside parking at start
Note	The route is not recommended for inexperienced walkers in poor visibility, when map and compass are essential.

All but one of the Howgills' major streams find their way into the Lune, although the one credited as being the river's source, on the basis that it has the longest passage to the sea, is Dale Gill. It seeps out of the rock below the summit of Green Bell and flows down to join the rivulets bubbling from Newbiggin's springs. Aficionados determined to walk the river in its entirety will follow the course of the peaty stream off the hill. However, more satisfying for those appreciative of striking landscape (and a drier path) is this more circuitous route, which ascends the eastern ridge defining Bowderdale and returns from Green Bell along its northern snout.

Leave the corner of the southbound slip road by its junction with the A685 at **Wath**, following a narrow lane signed as a Public Way. The tarmac ends at the entrance to **The Gars**, but the way continues through a gate ahead as an intermittently indistinct track across rough pasture. Eventually reaching the restored farmhouse at Cow Bank, it resumes as a lane. Descend towards the Weasdale Beck valley, but after 100m turn sharp right to double back across rough grazing, meeting a wall.

Follow the wall right, in time passing through a gate out of the intake. Where the wall later swings to the left, pick up a trod that rises across the eastern flank of **Hooksey** above Weasdale. Gaining height, the vista opens across to the Northern Pennines, while the buttress of West Grain divides the deepening valley ahead.

As the trod fades, maintain an

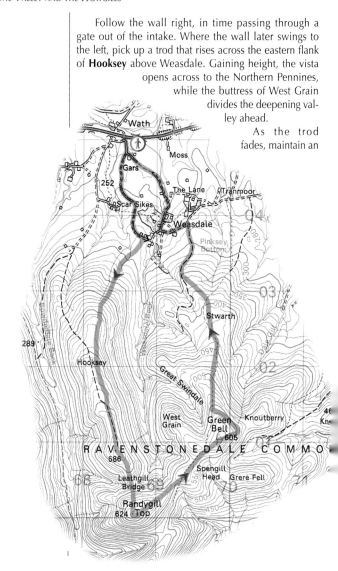

upward slant, soon joining a more distinct quad track. Continue along the rising crest, the views revealing the complex geography of the ridges and valleys of the Howgill massif, while the more distant scene ranges from Lakeland, on the one hand, to Wild Boar Fell. Beyond the high point, the ground abruptly falls to the narrow saddle of **Leathgill Bridge**. The steep climb beyond is soon accomplished, the gradient suddenly easing to reveal a small pile of stones marking the summit of **Randygill Top**.

> The greatest elevation of the walk, **Randygill Top**, is a marvellous vantage point. The panorama encompasses most of the major Lakeland peaks, while in the other direction, two of Yorkshire's Three Peaks are visible – the third, Pen-y-ghent, hides behind Baugh Fell. Cross Fell, the highest top of the Northern Pennines, lies to the north beyond the Eden Valley, but, being undistinguished by a transmitter, it is less distinctive than the nearer Great Dunn Fell.

A distinct trod descends north-east to another narrow waist of high ground separating the head of Weasdale from Stockless Gill. Gently climbing, carry on for another ½ mile (800m). Having passed the falling promontory of West Grain over to the left, watch for the path dividing. That to the left offers a short-cut above the head of Great Swindale, while the path ahead rises to the summit of **Green Bell**.

Although slightly lower than Randygill Top, Green Bell boasts a trig pillar. For survey purposes, it offered a better prospect to the eastern and northern hills, and it too is a grand tarrying place from which to enjoy the landscape.

To find the source of the Lune, keep with the path ahead, losing height fairly rapidly north-eastwards towards the much lower top of **Knoutberry**. As the gradient eases, bear off left, passing the ruin of a sheepfold and walking a short distance beyond it to find a couple of springs seeping from the ground.

Dale Gill is probably the least remarkable of the valleys cleaving the Howgills, with Langdale, Bowderdale and Weasdale all possessing much greater scenic appeal. But those wishing to trace the river's course will find a developing path above its right bank to take them down the valley. Later becoming a track, it eventually hits the lane just west of Greenside.

The way back to Wath, however, drops along the ridge running north from Green Bell. To avoid the climb back to the summit, contour north-west around the steep flank of the hill for ¼ mile (400m) to intersect the main path from the summit at a waypost. If you have time to spare, it is worth wandering back a short distance around the north-western slope of Green Bell for the views into the head of Great Swindale.

Return to the waypost and take the leftmost of the two descending paths, which bypasses left of **Stwarth**. Stay with the left branch past two more forks, and a track

On the summit of Green Bell

soon develops that winds above the intake wall and finally meets a lane east of **Weasdale**.

From the flanks of Green Bell into Great Swindale

To the left the lane heads down into the small settlement. There, take a bridleway on the right, which leads to Weasdale Nurseries. Keep ahead through a gate beside the front porch of Low Weasdale Cottage, walking forward through a second gate to join Weasdale Beck. Over a footbridge, continue through a gate beside a barn, remaining briefly with the river before moving away across the fields towards the house at **Gars**. Leave the corner of the penultimate field through the left gate, walking across to a small gate in the property's rear wall. The Right of Way winds through the yard, or, alternatively, follow the boundary left to the lane. Turn right back to **Wath**.

WALK 2
Newbiggin-on-Lune

Start Point	Ravenstonedale (NY 722 042)
Distance	6½ miles (10.5km)
Time	3hrs
Terrain	Field paths and disused railway
Height Gain	240m (787ft)
Maps	Explorer OL19 – Howgill Fells and Upper Eden Valley
Refreshments	Black Swan at Ravenstonedale, Lune Spring Garden Centre café in Newbiggin-on-Lune
Toilets	None
Parking	Parking in front of St Oswald's Church

This walk straddles the subtle watershed between Lunesdale and neighbouring Smardale, where Scandal Beck is one of the principal tributaries of the Eden, a northerly flowing river that enters the Solway Firth below Carlisle. The country here is underlain by limestone, its pale grey countenance reflected in the farm buildings, cottages and dry-stone walls that enclose the fields, but brightened in spring and summer by the flowers that abound in the hedgerows and banks. Beginning in Ravenstonedale, the walk crosses the fields to Newbiggin, where a spring is traditionally held to be the source of the Lune. Following the course of a former railway into the pretty valley of Smardale, it returns to the village past medieval earthworks.

ST OSWALD'S CHURCH, RAVENSTONEDALE

Ravenstonedale's churchyard is home to the village's most ancient monument, the base of a Saxon cross, indicating the existence of Christian settlement well before the arrival of the Normans. Towards the end of the 12th century, the manor was gifted to the Gilbertine priory at Watton in Yorkshire, part of the only religious order to have been founded by an Englishman.

The son of a Norman knight and born at Sempringham in Lincolnshire, Gilbert died in 1189, having lived to be over 100. He was revered for his piety and his work with women and the poor, and over 30 houses were established in his name, although the priory at Ravenstonedale is the only one known west of the Pennines.

The ruins, which lie beside the church, date from around 1200 and once housed a small community of canons and lay brethren. Little remains apart from the excavated foundations, and it is likely that when St Oswald's Church was rebuilt in 1744 the ruins were plundered as a convenient quarry of ready-cut stone.

A splendid building from the outside, the church is even more remarkable within, being one of few in the country that adopt the collegiate plan, where the pews face inward to a centre aisle. The most spectacular feature is undoubtedly the grand three-decker pulpit, rendered even more imposing by a massive sounding-board suspended above. It came from the earlier building and commands the attention of all.

From the front of **St Oswald's Church**, head into the village, following the lane signed to Sedbergh. At a junction by the Black Swan, turn right and then, at the next junction, fork right past a raised green. At the end, go right again to Town Head Farm. Bear left through a gate to pass beside cattle sheds and then bend left along a short

The interior layout of St Oswald's, unusually, is based on the collegiate plan

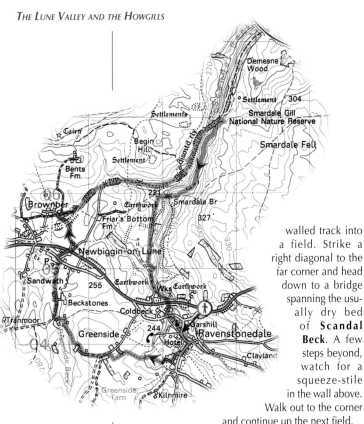

walled track into a field. Strike a right diagonal to the far corner and head down to a bridge spanning the usually dry bed of **Scandal Beck**. A few steps beyond, watch for a squeeze-stile in the wall above. Walk out to the corner and continue up the next field.

At the top, go left through a gate and follow the boundary away. To the south, beyond Greenside Tarn, the northern slopes of the Howgills rise to Green Bell, from whose flank springs Dale Gill, the Lune's most distant tributary from the sea. At a protruding stub of wall, part-way along the second field, swing right through a squeeze-gap towards a cottage. Wind left and right out of the fields onto a narrow lane.

Follow it left for ¼ mile (400m), leaving after the second cattle-grid for a stile on the right. Pass behind **High Greenside Farm**, crossing a succession of fences

to a wall-stile at its far side. Over that go right above
Greenside Beck. Entering the third field by a barn, turn
left to a bridge spanning the stream and leave the pasture
along a drive from a cottage. Newbiggin-on-Lune is signed
right beside the stream past a well-preserved lime kiln.

> The 18th century was an age of agricultural
> improvements, which included the use of lime as
> a fertiliser. Thousands of **field kilns** were built up
> and down the country, in which limestone was
> burned using culm, a poor quality coal, as a fuel.
> The process took a couple of days, after which the
> quicklime was raked out and left to weather before
> being laboriously spread over the fields to counter-
> act acidity in the soil.

At **Beckstones Farm**, cross a bridge to the other bank,
but where the track then shortly swings right, keep ahead
on a narrow path into thicket. Parting company with the
stream, mount a stile and walk the length of a field to meet
a lane at the edge of **Newbiggin-on-Lune**. Head towards
the village, but go right at the first junction to reach the
main road beside the Lune Spring Garden Centre. Taking
the narrow lane diagonally opposite, look over the left
wall to see a grass mound, the site of St Helen's Chapel,
and a stream that upwells beside it, the River Lune. A stile
a little further along gives access to the field.

> The perpetual spring of **St Helen's Well** was prob-
> ably revered long before the arrival of Christianity
> and, as was often the case, adopted by the new
> religion with the foundation of a chapel. The resur-
> gence has traditionally been regarded as the true
> source of the Lune, a Celtic name meaning 'pure' or
> 'healthy'. St Helen was the mother of Constantine I,
> the first Roman emperor to embrace Christianity,
> and she was credited with discovering the 'true
> cross' on which Christ was crucified.

Cross the field, through which runs a second stream, to a track at the far side and follow it right beneath a disused railway bridge to a junction at the entrance to **Brownber Hall**. Turn right again, the way signed to Smardale. Winding past a barn, meet the course of the Stainmore Railway, which ran across the Pennines between Tebay and Darlington. Join the former railway through a gate on the left, shortly passing the ruin of Sandy Bank signal box, which marked the summit separating Lunesdale and Smardale. The line runs on into a cutting, the banks resplendent in spring with wood anemone, celandine, coltsfoot, primrose, cowslip and violet. After passing beneath a bridge, its parapet still blackened by soot, the track winds past an abandoned limestone quarry and kilns before curving across an impressive **viaduct** straddling the gorge.

SMARDALE QUARRY AND SMARDALE GILL VIADUCT

The quarry opened shortly after the Stainmore Railway in 1861, providing stone for the massive lime kilns that were built beside the track. The unprecedented industrial expansion and urbanisation of the 19th century created a huge demand for burnt lime, since it was used not only for fertiliser but also for mortar and cement and in the production of glass and the smelting of iron. The lime here was destined for the steelworks at Barrow and Darlington, but the quality proved inferior, and the quarry was abandoned before the end of the 19th century.

The viaduct, a little further along, was an impressive demonstration of Victorian engineering, its 14 arches spanning 168m and carrying the track 27m above the river. It was built with the foresight to accommodate twin lines as traffic increased, but although much of the route was soon upgraded to two-way operation, the section here remained single track. With the closure of the Barrow steelworks in 1961, the line was shut and the rails removed, along with several viaducts, including that across the River Belah, which lay 9 miles (14.5km) to the east. At 60m high, it was the tallest bridge in Britain. The Smardale Gill Viaduct almost shared the same fate, for by 1980 its condition had deteriorated to the point of becoming dangerous. However, British Rail offered a grant reflecting the cost of demolition for its restoration, and the bridge was re-opened in 1992 as a link to the Smardale Nature Reserve along the valley.

On the far side of the viaduct leave over a stile on the right, from which a path runs back up the valley, giving a superb retrospective view to the viaduct. After passing the limestone quarries over on the other side, watch for a fork and climb to a stile above. Those with their noses to the ground will have noticed the rock underfoot change from limestone to sandstone, which was cut from the hillside a little further along for the construction of the viaduct. Beyond the quarries, cross a stile and follow a bridleway down to **Smardale Bridge**.

Climb away to a stile a short distance up on the left and head out across the hillside to meet a low earthen dyke. It was part of a boundary enclosing the valley and was raised by monks from the small Gilbertine priory at Ravenstonedale to protect their timber and fishing rights. The hillside terraces above are lynchets, which were created by medieval strip ploughing. Follow the dyke past the end of a stand of timber above a narrowing of the gorge. Later, the path loses height across an open field, where low grass pillow-mounds are the remains of conies or warrens, built during the Middle Ages to encourage

The Smardale Gill Viaduct is an impressive example of Victorian engineering

breeding rabbits to provide a ready source of meat. At the far end, posts mark the path down a steep bank to a footbridge across a side-stream from Hag Mire.

Walk up to join a rising track towards Park House, but after 100m branch down beside a fence. Through gates, cross a second track coming from a bridge and carry on past a byre beside the river. Through a gate on the right by a footbridge join the adjacent track and follow it beneath the road bridge into **Ravenstonedale**. Reaching the main lane, cross Coldbeck Bridge, and at the junction immediately beyond bear right between buildings, from which a path leads across a playing field back to St Oswald's Church.

WALK 3
Wath to Kelleth

Start Point	Wath (NY 684 049)
Distance	4 miles (6.4km)
Time	1¾hrs
Terrain	Field paths and quiet lanes
Height Gain	105m (344ft)
Maps	Explorer OL19 – Howgill Fells and Upper Eden Valley
Refreshments	Lune Spring Garden Centre café, Newbiggin-on-Lune
Toilets	None
Parking	Roadside parking at start

Set in a wide valley between Great Asby Scar and the northern extremities of the Howgills, the upper reaches of the Lune's valley provide lush grazing for cattle and sheep. The main road commandeers the base of the valley, following the embankment built for the Stainmore Railway. However, set further back, field paths and peaceful lanes invite relaxed rambling, with fine views to the wider backdrop of hills. This walk links the hamlets of Kelleth and Wath, both founded as farming settlements.

The **Stainmore Railway** ran between Darlington and Tebay and was completed in 1861. A strategic east–west route, the line was built by the South Durham & Lancashire Union Railway to transport Durham coke to the steelworks at Furness, and then return with high quality hematite needed for steel production on the Tees. Crossing the Pennines through the Stainmore Gap, the railway's summit at 457m (1370ft) was the highest of any English main line and, being a particularly scenic route, it helped popularise the Lancashire seaside resorts as a destination for those in the north-east. However, the line remained predominantly used for freight, and after the demise of the Barrow steel industry in 1961 it was closed and the track taken up.

Join the minor lane, which burrows beneath the A685 bypass at **Wath**, and follow it south towards Bowderdale and Scar Sykes. At a fork take the **Bowderdale** branch to the right. Cross the stream at Bowderdale Foot and carry on along the lane to the farm at **Long Gill**. Passing through the gate, swing left in front of the farmhouse and then right through more gates beside the buildings and garden. Entering the field behind, go half-right to the foot of a gully. Veer left through a gate and walk on, with a fence now on your left. Approaching the far side of the second field, bear right and leave over a bridge onto a track. Follow it left to **Flakebridge Farm**.

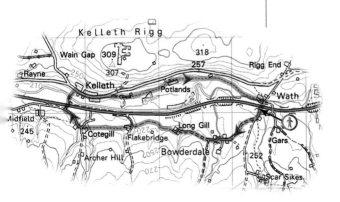

Passing the corner of the 18th-century farmhouse, take a gate on the right into a small yard. Walk ahead through a second gate, entering the field beyond by yet another gate. Head away beside the wall towards the next farm, **Cotegill**.

Walk through the yard to reach a lane and go forward past the old farmhouse. Later reaching a junction, turn right to the main road. Cross to a gate beside the house opposite and pick up a grass track that winds through a second gate and leads down to a footbridge spanning the River Lune. A hollow path takes the way uphill to meet a lane at the edge of **Kelleth**.

Turn right through the village, passing the attractive 17th-century Kelleth Old Hall. Until 1978 it remained in the hands of a single family, the Whiteheads, who had been associated with George Fox, the founder of the Quaker Movement.

At the far end of the village, fork right through a gate along a track signed to Wath. Pass through a couple of gates at the end and continue across the fields towards a tall barn. It was built into the slope of the hill so that its upper hayloft could be more easily filled to feed cattle,

Kelleth Old Hall

which were over-wintered in the stalls below. Having
passed above a wood bear left, gaining height to a stile
in the next wall. Keep going above **Potlands Farm**, eventually leaving the fields at **Wath**. Walk out through the
farmyard to the lane and go right, crossing the Lune to
return to the start.

WALK 4
Bowderdale and The Calf

Start Point	Bowderdale (NY 678 046)
Distance	11 miles (17.7km)
Time	5½hrs
Terrain	Valley paths and upland grass trods
Height Gain	605m (1985ft)
Maps	Explorer OL19 – Howgill Fells and Upper Eden Valley
Refreshments	Nearest facilities at Tebay
Toilets	None
Parking	Laneside parking near bridge at Bowderdale Foot
Note	The route is not recommended for inexperienced walkers in poor visibility, when map and compass are essential.

Viewed from Sedbergh, the routes onto The Calf appear uncompromisingly
steep, but approached from the north, gentle ridges and extended valleys
suggest a less demanding path to the highest top of the Howgills. Long and
straight, delving into the heart of the hills, Bowderdale is a wonderfully
secluded place, where often you will have only fell ponies and the odd
buzzard soaring overhead for company. The return over Hazelgill Knott
gives dramatic glimpses into the upper reaches of Langdale, revealing the
secretive folded beauty of the valley heads. If you are only to do one walk in
the Howgills, this should be it.

A bridleway into Bowderdale leaves left from the lane,
200m west of the bridge at **Bowderdale Foot**. Follow the

43

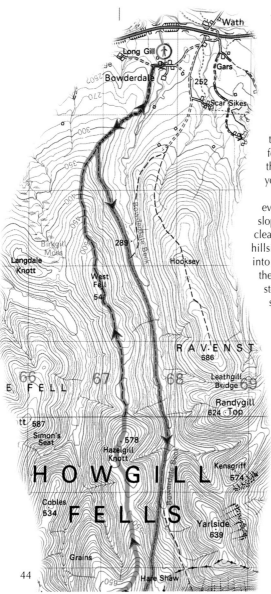

track through a couple of gates to the corner of a conifer plantation. It then curves across rough pasture, gaining height to a final gate in the far corner. Carry on beside a gently rising wall at the edge of the open fell, with the mouth of the long valley drawing you forwards.

Where the wall eventually turns down the slope, keep ahead on the clear path, contouring the hillside above the stream into the valley. Although the view is contained by steep, grassy flanks, the scenery is magnificent, striking for both the dale's straightness and the squirming of the silvery beck along its base. The path meanders on, crossing occasional springs that tumble from above, and eventually passes the confluence where **Randy Gill** joins the main stream. Yarlside rises boldly between the two, an impressive hill topping 630m (over

44

map continues on page 45

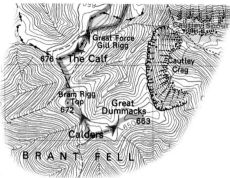

2000ft) and the highest of the eastern group of Howgill summits.

Keep going as the higher reaches of the dale now appear, eventually crossing Rams Gill, the last spring to be encountered during the day. Beyond, the path begins a measured, plodding ascent, steadily rising across the slope above **Hare Shaw** to bring the crumbling edge of Cautley Crag into view. Higher up, the path finally turns its back on Bowderdale, climbing above Swere Gill and Red Gill Beck, the two streams that feed the famous waterfall of Cautley Spout, although from this walk the cascade remains unseen.

In time, the path levels to a junction by a couple of small tarns, bringing into view the distant Lakeland hills. The way curves to the left above the head of **Langdale**, which lies down to the right. Keep left at an indistinct fork and make for the white trig pillar marking the summit of **The Calf**, beside which, perhaps surprisingly, there is another, larger tarn occupying a shallow scrape on the plateau.

> The view from the summit of **The Calf** is grand. To the west the distant high peaks of Lakeland form a ragged horizon –The Old Man of Coniston, Scafell and Scafell Pike, Great Gable and Helvellyn can all be distinguished. To the south-east among the hills of the Dales are the Yorkshire Three Peaks – Pen-y-ghent, Whernside and Ingleborough, while closer to is Baugh Fell, with Swarth Fell, Wild Boar Fell and Nine Standards Rigg panning around to the east. Down below, the Lune Viaduct, built to carry the Ingleton Railway, marks the foot of the Lune Gorge.

In clear weather, the temptation to explore the nearby tops can prove irresistible, for each offers its own perspective of the scene. Calders lies to the south beyond Bram Rigg Top, and the broad ridge then arcs east to Great Dummacks. The walk there and back will add a further 2½ miles (4km) to the day, but it is not difficult, and there is no great loss of height involved.

To return from the summit of The Calf, retrace your steps to the tarns passed on the way up, paying particular attention to navigation if visibility is poor. Ignore the faint trod leaving just before the pools, which heads more or less due north and follows the descending rigg of Grains into Langdale. Instead walk past the first of the two tarns and then branch left immediately beyond it. The path initially heads north-east, later bending to the north as it settles along the grassy ridge separating East Grain from Bowderdale. The next mile or so is one of the highlights of the whole walk and gives a superb prospect of the complex ridges and valleys that buttress the northern Howgill plateau.

Yarlside rises impressively towards the head of Bowderdale

Now obvious, the path loses height to a shallow saddle before rising again over **Hazelgill Knott**, which

deserves a brief halt to take stock of the panorama. Beyond, the route drops once more to another saddle before tackling the last rise onto **West Fell**. There is another commanding view, this time over the foot of the dale. The final leg is a long gentle descent, which looks out to the neat fields on the limestone slopes of Great Asby Scar. Ultimately closing with a wall, retrace your outward steps to **Bowderdale Foot**.

Gazing across East Grain to Simon's Seat

47

WALK 5
Gaisgill to Orton

Start Point	Gaisgill (NY 640 053)
Distance	6½ miles (10.5km)
Time	3hrs
Terrain	Field paths and lanes
Height Gain	165m (541ft)
Maps	Explorer OL19 – Howgill Fells and Upper Eden Valley
Refreshments	Tea room and pub in Orton
Toilets	Orton
Parking	Roadside parking in Gaisgill

The attractive village of Orton sits below the bare limestone plateau of Great Asby Scar, not far from the first major confluence of the River Lune, where it is joined by Birk Beck before swinging south to define the western boundary of the Howgills. This pleasant countryside ramble to the village from the Luneside settlement of Gaisgill explores a short stretch of the river and encounters some of the pretty, contributing becks that resurge from the foot of the limestone upland.

Walk out to the main road in **Gaisgill**, going right and then left along a side-lane signed to Raisbeck and Kelleth. After crossing Langdale Beck, the lane winds around to **Rayne Bridge** spanning the Lune. Once over, take the short field track on the left, but immediately go through a gate on the right. A trod climbs away by the left fence to a squeeze-stile. Continue above a wooded bank and then contour the slope of the hill from field to field, eventually reaching the farm at **Raisgill Hall**. Pass through the yard to a lane.

Cross diagonally right to a field gate, from which a field path is signed to Orton. Strike out half-right to find a stile in the wall behind a complex of cowsheds and head away across the next pasture to a gate in the far fence.

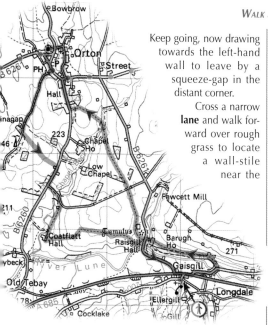

Keep going, now drawing towards the left-hand wall to leave by a squeeze-gap in the distant corner.

Cross a narrow **lane** and walk forward over rough grass to locate a wall-stile near the

The Lakeland hills form a backdrop to lower Lunesdale

49

*All Saints Church
at Orton*

corner of a belt of woodland. Walk away on a left diagonal, continuing the line across a second field and aiming
for the right-hand edge of a wall at the far side. Over the
stile there, keep going to the far-left corner by more trees.
Pass through a gate into the trees and bear right down a
bank to then follow **Chapel Beck** up to a bridge.

Ignore the track on the far bank and instead go
through the gate opposite. Head half-right across a
large field to the walled corner of a wood. With the wall
on your right, walk forward to emerge through a gate onto a
lane. Turn right towards the village past the 17th-century
Orton Hall, set back within its grounds.

Reaching a junction at the edge of the village of
Orton, go right along a lane signed to Raisbeck. However,
immediately over a bridge spanning Chapel Beck, turn

WALK 5 – GAISGILL TO ORTON

off left on a back lane. It eventually swings left back to the main lane. Cross to the metalled track opposite that leads up to **All Saints Church**.

> In the 12th century **All Saints Church** was held by Conishead Priory, far away, overlooking the sands of Morecambe Bay near Ulverston. Byland Abbey, even more distant in Yorkshire, also possessed lands in the area. The present structure dates from the 13th century, although, in common with most other churches, it has been much altered over the centuries. Inside are listed the incumbents who oversaw those changes. Among the church's treasures is a display of ancient bells hanging from their headstocks, a sturdy font of red sandstone bearing the date of 1622, and a simple chest, rough-hewn from a single tree trunk, which required three separate keyholders for its opening to ensure the integrity of the parish records. Eight more bells hang within the tower, whose creamy rendering is seemingly at odds with the rest of the building, but is a reversion to the original lime plaster needed to keep out the damp.

Just beyond the church, go left to a junction, beside which are found the village stocks in which miscreants were left to ponder on their sins. Keep ahead through the market place to rejoin the main lane opposite the **George Hotel**.

ORTON

Still a lively focus for the area, Orton was first granted a market charter by Edward I. Its scope was extended by Oliver Cromwell, who licensed Whitsun fairs. These must have been boisterous affairs, for the title also authorised a piepowder court. Deriving from the French *pieds poudrés*, meaning 'dusty feet', they were an efficient means of resolving disputes and dealing with any unruly behaviour or crime that occurred during the course of the fair. Speed was of the essence, since the fair drew crowds from far and wide, who would be long gone after the last day. Punishments for petty offences took the form of fines, seizure of goods, time in the stocks or being paraded around the town in humiliation.

Walk on away from the village, but then turn off beside the **Orton Liberal Club**, built in 1888 and fronted by a small garden. Swing left and then right to follow a narrow, old walled track, Martinagap Lane. Where the walls end after ½ mile (800m), by a cottage at **Martinagap**, leave through small gate on the left. Follow the left boundary and then pass through a gate before striking half-right across a field to a cottage, which appears by the far corner as you crest the rise.

Emerge beside it onto the **B6260** and go right. After 250m, turn off left along a narrow lane, which meanders down to cross **Chapel Beck** at Coatflatt Bridge. Carry on a further 100m before leaving over a stile beside the entrance to Coatflatt Mill. Through a gate, walk at the field edge past the cottage. Beyond another gate, continue beside a wall, eventually joining a track. Keep ahead past a bridge and then branch left through a gate to pass the converted buildings of **Coatflatt Hall**.

Where the track swings right at the far end of the buildings, turn through a gate on the left. Follow a field track across a ditch, and then bear left to join a wall. Negotiating an opening at the top, bear half-left to a gap at the far corner. Wind into a small enclosure, leaving through a gate to walk away, with a wall on your right. Passing into another pen, exit by the second gate on your right and, with the wall now on your left, follow it around to a gate at the far end. Cross a final meadow to reach the lane opposite **Raisgill Hall**.

You can either return by your outward route, which lies just to the left, or go right, following the lane over Raisgill Hall Bridge and back to the main road opposite **Gaisgill**.

WALK 6
Orton Scar

Start Point	Orton (NY 622 082)
Distance	7 miles (11.3km)
Time	3¼hrs
Terrain	Field paths and limestone pavement
Height Gain	270m (886ft)
Maps	Explorer OL19 – Howgill Fells and Upper Eden Valley
Refreshments	Tea room and pub in Orton
Toilets	Orton
Parking	Car park by Orton Market Hall

The limestone pavements of the Orton Fells are amongst the most extensive in England and sweep for some 5 miles (8km) across the northern hilltops above upper Lunesdale. Striking scenery, a rich variety of plant and birdlife, and evocative relics of man's prehistoric presence are the highlights of this superb walk from the attractive village of Orton.

From the car park behind **Orton** Market Hall in the centre of the village, go uphill and take the narrow lane to the church. Swinging right, walk down to the main road, cross it and carry on past the vicarage. Turn left just before the stream, and then left again after 100m along a drive between houses, curving right to pick up an old walled path. Stay with the right-hand boundary as the track briefly opens before resuming as a greenway beside a crystal-clear stream. Eventually passing through a gate by a junction of streams, strike upfield to **Broadfell Farm**.

Pass left of the buildings and keep going uphill by the left boundary, passing a lime kiln near the top before finally coming out onto a lane. Turn right over a cattle-grid and immediately leave right to climb away onto the open hill beside the right-hand wall. Breasting a low scar, the monument marking the summit of **Beacon Hill** comes into view.

As its name suggests, the fell is an old **beacon hill**, where a fire would have been lit to warn of approaching Scots cattle thieves. The monument is a more recent affair, erected to commemorate the Golden Jubilee of Queen Victoria in 1887. The cross was carved by a local farmer and self-taught sculptor from Reagill, Thomas Bland. The raised lead lettering has long since gone, but the loyal inscription can still be made out.

Carry on beside the wall, ignoring a metal gate and continuing within a shallow corner to a second gate. Pass through to continue on the other side of the wall for a further 250m to find a large boulder incorporated within it, the **Thunder Stone**. It is an erratic boulder of pink granite, which was carried from Shap Fell by an ice sheet. Return to the gate and, without passing through, bear left from the wall on a trod. Over the crest, bear left again, descending to a gate in a wall by a four-way signpost.

Stay on this side and go left, the bridleway gradually diverging from the wall to meet another

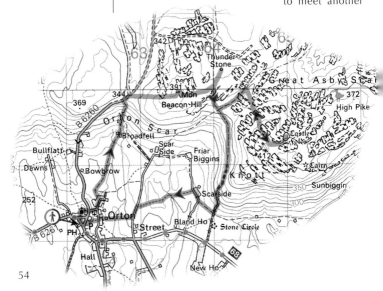

Castle Folds settlement

wall at a gate onto the Great Asby Scar Nature Reserve. Passing through, turn right and follow the path by the wall (initially indistinct) at the edge of an extensive limestone pavement, gently climbing towards the top of the hill. Reaching a junction of walls, scale a ladder-stile and strike half-left across the fractured rock towards a low, sloping platform, **Castle Folds**. Care is needed as some of the clints (blocks) are loose, and the grikes (or crevices) between them can be deep.

> At **Castle Folds** collapsed rubble walls mark the perimeter of an extensive Romano-British settlement site, which at one time would have stood around 3m high. Inside, the positions of a number of buildings can be identified and suggest a thriving community. The area has been settled since Mesolithic times, with flints and axe heads being found at several locations. The hills were farmed from the Bronze Age onwards, and copper ore was mined nearby.

Return to climb the ladder-stile. Without scaling the adjacent high wall, there is no way to reach the trig column on the other side, so instead, retrace your steps back to the gate at the entrance to the nature reserve and then to the four-way signpost encountered earlier. This time, turn left through the gate and follow a green path that contours the slope below **Knott**. Later, as the path descends more steeply, there is a view to the **Gamelands Stone Circle** in the corner of a field below. Drop from the open hill through a gate by a lime kiln.

The tower of Orton's church serves as a guide back to the village

Although some stones are undoubtedly missing, **Gamelands Stone Circle** still comprises some 40 boulders, all but one being erratics of pink Shap granite. They toppled in antiquity, but remain an impressive sight, forming a slightly flattened ring some 45m at its greatest diameter. It is the largest such monument in Cumbria and was erected around 1800–1400BC, at about the time that bronze was introduced into Britain. Such sites do not usually contain either burials or dwellings and are assumed to have been a focus for ceremony or gathering, although their true purpose will, perhaps, forever remain a mystery.

Some 200m beyond the lime kiln, pass through a gateway on the right, from which a bridleway is signed to Scarside. Walk parallel with the right-hand fence towards **Scarside Farm**, passing out beside it onto a narrow lane. Go right, but leave through a gate opposite the farmhouse, from which a sign marks a path to Street Lane. Carry on from field to field, shortly crossing a brook. Now tending to the left wall, keep going across more fields, ultimately emerging onto **Street Lane**.

Walk left for 150m to find a stile beside a power-line post. Head away towards **Orton**, the white church tower now serving as a guide. Exit the field corner by a cottage and follow a narrow path out to a lane. Cross the stream to continue along a metalled path opposite beside a playing field back into the village.

WALK 7
Birk Beck

Start Point	Greenholme (NY 597 057)
Distance	5½ miles (8.9km)
Time	2½hrs
Terrain	Rough lowland moor, indistinct paths
Height Gain	175m (574ft)
Maps	Explorer OL7 – English Lakes (South Eastern area)
Refreshments	Nearest facilities at Orton
Toilets	Orton
Parking	Roadside parking in Greenholme

Birk Beck is the most northerly of the Lune's many tributaries and comes down from the upper flanks of Great Yarlside among the Shap Fells. It flows across a lonely, open moor, from which there are fine views to the slopes of the Howgills. The walk follows the beck's course from the hamlet of Greenholme before returning across the hillside.

From the junction in **Greenholme** take the lane crossing the bridge over Birk Beck towards Orton. Climb away for some 200m and then leave through a gate on the left, from which a path is signed to Steps. Follow the direction of the fingerpost, later dropping to a footbridge at the bottom of a steep bank. Carry on towards a stone stile in the far corner and maintain the line across the next field to another stile at the left end of the far wall. Continue beside the stream to the farm at **Steps**, joining its track, which shortly crosses Birk Beck to meet a lane.

Follow the lane upstream, recrossing the beck before reaching **Scout Green**. Beyond the cottages, the lane climbs to a sharp bend, where you take the track to the left, signed to Salterwath. After 150m, at a way-post, veer off right across the rough moorland, aiming north-west to pick up a quad track. Nearing a barn, move left to find a stile in the corner by the river.

Paralleling the river along the top of a bank, carry on beside a collapsed wall. Approaching a small **wood**, cross the right-hand fence and immediately go left to a stone stile. The way continues above the wood, but the beck is hidden at the foot of the precipitous bank, where it tumbles over the small but impressive Docker Force.

Eventually, the fence falls away, but keep ahead, shortly meeting a stone step-stile in a lateral wall. Now in pasture, parallel a fence over to the right while ascending a bank towards a lone sycamore.

There bear left over the rise towards **Salterwath Farm**, which then comes into view. Leave the field through a small gate in the wall to its right.

Birk Beck near Salterwath

Head left along a track past the farm buildings, forking left beyond them over a bridge. Gaining height, follow the track away, watching for a stile, some 250m along on the left. Strike half-right towards **Stonygill Farm**, passing behind the buildings. Through a gate bear left, dropping to a footbridge at the bottom of a bank. Climb beyond and walk to a stile, and over this go right.

Walk past a derelict barn but, contrary to what is shown on the OS map, remain on this side of the wall. Mount a ladder-stile in the corner and keep going by the boundary, soon passing the abandoned steading of Gibsonhill. Keep with the wall as it then swings left, but later move away when it curves right. Picking up a vague track, descend across the slope of the valley towards **Rampshowe**, which shortly comes into view ahead. Through a couple of gates, pass below the farmhouse to emerge onto a track. Follow it away to the right, later crossing Stakeley Beck before reaching **Gill Farm**.

Walk past the front of the barn and adjoining house, leaving through a small metal gate into the rough pasture beyond. Continue across the hillside to a stile and then clamber down a bank to cross a stream. Climb out to find a fence-stile on the right and walk away, hugging a wall at the edge of the rising moor. After passing above Whitebrow, join a track, which soon crosses a stream. There, fork right along a grass track that runs out to the bend of a lane.

Follow it ahead past the farm at **Ewelock Bank**, but as it then bends right in a dip, leave at a footpath sign pointing left to Greenholme. Walk down to a stile in the corner of a wall, noticing to the right a lime kiln. It was built into the slope of the bank to facilitate loading at the top and emptying from the bottom. Bear right to a fence-stile and continue downhill above a small stream. Through a gate, join a second stream and carry on down to join yet another beck. Over that, take a path right, negotiating a couple of wall-stiles and eventually reaching a footbridge behind a farm. Cross the bridge and follow the path over a final stile to emerge onto the lane back at **Greenholme**.

WALK 8
Bretherdale

Start Point	Greenholme (NY 597 057)
Distance	5 miles (8km)
Time	2½hrs
Terrain	Rough field paths, tracks and lane
Height Gain	225m (738ft)
Maps	Explorer OL7 – English Lakes (South Eastern area)
Refreshments	Nearest facilities at Orton
Toilets	Orton
Parking	Roadside parking in Greenholme

Bretherdale is one of those delightful backwaters that, despite its beauties, has become largely forgotten. In days past, it was a through-route from the head of the Lune Gorge to the west, and two tracks climb from its higher reaches – one leads into neighbouring Borrowdale, while the other rises at the head of the valley to meet the Kendal to Shap road above Crookdale. This shorter walk explores the valley's middle reaches, having first climbed the hill on its northern side, which offers a fine prospect into its heart.

From the junction in **Greenholme**, take the lane north towards Shap, but immediately turn off left on a track between a cottage and the former schoolhouse, which is signed to Bretherdale Head. At **Low Whinhowe Farm**, keep on through a gate and cross a stream. Fork right by a tumbledown building and follow a hollow path parallel to the stream.

The track from Greenholme to Low Whinhowe

Through a gate at the top, where stunted apple trees pervade the hedge, walk on across open pasture, ignoring the crossing track to the abandoned farm at High Whinhowe. Carry on over the rise through a couple more gates. As a track develops, stay with the left branch to intersect a narrow lane.

The onward route lies along the bridleway opposite, but for the view it is worth first climbing the hill topped by a survey pillar facing you. Bear right across a marshy area to round the corner of the wall, and there pick up a firmer trod beside it to the top. The trig column is not the highest point – that lies a short distance further on – but between the two of them they give a marvellous panorama across the surrounding countryside.

Reference to your map shows that from here it is possible to continue above the wall for a further ¼ mile (400m) and then follow a narrow strip of access land into the bottom of the valley. However, this involves scaling several unstiled boundaries and misses one of the prettiest sections of the walk. Therefore, retrace your steps to the lane and follow the bridleway

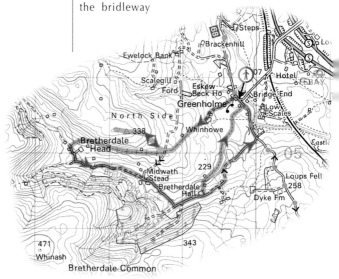

through a gate along the valley side. The track eventually winds down to **Bretherdale Beck**, where a cantilevered slab bridge provides a dry-footed crossing. Walk past the ruined **Bretherdale Head Farm**, joining a farm track and crossing Breasthigh Beck to meet a narrow lane.

A glimpse through the trees to Bretherdale Head

Follow the lane left down the valley for a good ½ mile (800m), recrossing the beck into the tiny settlement of **Midwath Stead**. Ahead, the lane carries on, later reverting to the southern slopes, where it gains height to give a superb back-view along the dale. The lane swings sharply left and continues to **Bretherdale Hall**.

Here there are two options – simply follow the lane for a further ¾ mile (1.2km) to its end and turn left back to **Greenholme** or, alternatively, take to the fields. The latter, however, involves fording the stream and, unless the weather has been dry, can mean wet feet.

For the cross-country route, just past Bretherdale Hall, cross a stile in the left fence and walk down beside the end of the buildings. Over another stile, continue downhill on a hollow way to emerge above a cottage. Following the drive left and then right, skirt the cottage to pick up a path down to **Bretherdale Beck**.

On the far bank, bear right past a ruined farm, appropriately named Waters, and walk downstream. Through a gate, the path remains high above the beck. However, beyond a second gate, the stream turns away. Follow a wall to another gate and keep ahead across the remaining fields. A developing track leads past a restored barn to the lane. Go left back to the start at **Greenholme**.

WALK 9
Blease Fell

Start Point	Mount Pleasant, Tebay (NY 618 045)
Distance	6 miles (9.7km)
Time	3hrs
Terrain	Tracks and upland grass trods
Height Gain	325m (1066ft)
Maps	Explorer OL19 – Howgill Fells and Upper Eden Valley
Refreshments	Tea shop and pubs in Tebay
Toilets	Tebay Services
Parking	Roadside parking in Tebay
Note	While the ascent presents few navigational challenges, the return, particularly in poor visibility, demands care, and map and compass are essential.

A relatively easy walk onto the grass moors of Tebay Fell, which on its outward leg affords fine views across the Lune Valley to Jeffrey's Mount and Grayrigg Pike behind. The scenic climax, however, is from the snout of Blease Fell, where the abruptly falling hillside reveals a dramatic vision of the deep defile of Carlin Gill.

THE LUNE GORGE

The Lune Gorge served as a route north for the Romans, and its control remained important during the medieval period to deter Scottish raiding parties. A motte-and-bailey castle was established at the head of the gorge opposite the Lune's confluence with Birk Beck, and in the 12th century was held by the de Tybai family, from whom the settlement that grew beside it took its name. Tebay assumed some importance with the coming of the turnpikes in 1760, but it was the arrival of the railway that put the place on the map, the original village adopting the prefix 'Old' to distinguish it from the new settlement that sprang up above the station.

The Lancaster–Carlisle Railway, later incorporated within the LNWR, opened in 1846, with Tebay developing as an important junction when the Stainmore Railway brought a line from Darlington in 1861. A complex of goods sidings and sheds was built to marshal wagons bringing iron ore from Furness and coal from Teeside and to house engines used to assist northbound trains up to Shap summit. Cross-Pennine traffic steadily diminished after the war, and the Stainmore line finally closed in 1962, with the station and goods yard being subsequently removed.

In **Tebay** begin from the junction of the A685 with a minor lane at the top of the 'new' village, briefly following the lane past the Old School towards Gaisgill. Turn right immediately beyond onto a narrow lane leading onto the open fell. Keep right at two successive forks, picking up a sign to Tebay Gill. A little further on, at yet another fork, bear off left on a gravel track, which shortly passes a cottage, **Tebaygill**. The track becomes more rugged as it gains height above the deepening clough of Tebay Gill, and, looking back, there is a view to Great Asby Scar and the distant transmitter on Great Dun Fell.

Some ¼ mile (400m) beyond Tebaygill, passing the low mound of **Roger Howe**, branch right to follow an indistinct shepherd's quad-bike track. It gently rises along the broad grassy ridge that extends to the south, the increasing height revealing the hills bounding the western side of the Lune Valley – Jeffrey's Mount and the forbidding dark combs of Grayrigg Pike. The faint trod

A small cairn stands aside from the summit of Blease Fell overlooking the Lune Gorge

meanders on for 1¾ miles (2.8km) over a couple of false summits, eventually topping out on **Blease Fell**.

A bare, grassy expanse, **Blease Fell** summit is unremarkable – even its diminutive cairn sits to one side as if to avoid intruding upon the emptiness. But the wider view transcends all – gaze into the valley below, where railway, road and motorway (not to mention underground pipelines) vie with the river for space within the narrow gorge. The first road was built by the Romans to link the major forts at Lancaster and Penrith and was controlled by a camp established at the foot of Borrowdale. By the time the motorway was built, space had run out, and to make way a 1½-mile stretch of the A685 had to be realigned higher up the side of the valley. For an even more dramatic view, wander beyond the summit to the head of the steep abruptness of its southern flank. Far below lie the dark, winding cleft of Carlin Gill and the forbidding gash of Black Force, with the puckered ridges behind rising to the highest tops of the Howgill plateau.

With no clear paths, it is easy to become disoriented, and the unwary might be drawn along a quad trail across the shallow saddle above the head of Eller Gill towards Rispa Pike. Instead set your compass on a bearing just east of north towards **Hare Shaw**. Before long a faint track

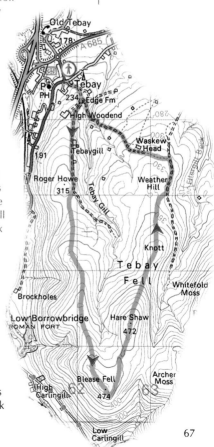

Across Eller Gill to Uldale End

develops that leads over the low summit, marked by a small pile of stones, and on along the descending ridge, which pinches before reaching Knott to give views into the valleys either side. Carry on over **Knott**, losing height towards the vague lump of **Weather Hill** – the name presumably derived from 'wether', a castrated sheep.

The quick way back is to strike out over Weather Hill and head straight for the farm at Waskew Head beyond. However, follow the tractor trail that veers right of the high point, dropping to join a rough stony track that opens views into Eller Gill. When the track shortly closes with a stone wall, carry on for nearly ¼ mile (400m), looking for an orienteering waypost set on the right-hand verge – if you reach a fence and gateway you have gone about 300m too far. Head out just north of west across the rough grass tussock. At first there is no obvious path, but on broaching the shoulder of the hill a trod develops towards the farm at **Waskew Head**, which then comes into view.

Leave along the farm's access track, which winds down to a bridge over **Tebay Gill**. Climbing over the shoulder of the hill beyond, it merges with other fell tracks to lead you back down to **Tebay**.

WALK 10

Jeffrey's Mount and Borrowdale

Start Point	Lune's Bridge, 1 mile (1.6km) south of Tebay (NY 613 028)
Distance	7¾ miles (12.5km)
Time	4hrs
Terrain	Upland grass trods and valley tracks and paths
Height Gain	530m (1739ft)
Maps	Explorer OL7 – English Lakes (South Eastern area) and Explorer OL19 – Howgill Fells and Upper Eden Valley
Refreshments	Nearest facilities at Tebay
Toilets	Tebay Services
Parking	Off-road parking at Lune's Bridge
Note	In poor visibility, care is needed in navigating the upland section, and map and compass are essential.

Less well known than its Lakeland namesake and consequently much less visited, Borrowdale – the valley of Borrow Beck – is a serenely pretty dale. Squeezed between the upland commons of Roundthwaite and Whinfell, the dale ushers its babbling stream to a confluence with the River Lune at Low Borrowbridge, near the site of a Roman fort. This walk explores the valley's middle reaches, having first looked down upon its secretive course from the high grassy ridge between Jeffrey's Mount and Belt Howe.

Initial proposals for Britain's **motorway** network were made in 1936, but it was not until 1958 that the country's first section of motorway opened, the 8¼-mile (13.3km) Preston by-pass. Construction continued piecemeal, with the section through the Lune Gorge to link Lancaster and Carlisle begun in 1967. To make way for the new road, it was necessary to realign 1½ miles (2.4km) of the existing A685 higher up the western flank of the valley below Jeffrey's Mount. The old road was truncated at Lune's Bridge and a new viaduct built to span the river, railway and motorway. The motorway was opened in 1970, and in 2010 it topped a poll to determine Britain's prettiest road.

From **Lune's Bridge** follow the main road over the viaduct before turning right along a lane to **Roundthwaite**. After nearly ½ mile (800m), bear off left along a bridleway signed to Borrowdale. The track rises above the settlement of Roundthwaite Abbey, which is considered more likely to have been an outlying grange rather than an abbey itself. At a crossing of tracks, keep left to climb more steeply to a gate.

The bridleway continues beside the wall along the flank of the broad valley containing Roundthwaite Beck, eventually ascending over a grassy pass in the lee of Belt Howe into Borrowdale. However, a more interesting route lies along the ridge, giving stunning views to the surrounding hills. For this, leave the bridleway just beyond the gate on a faint path that begins a steady climb onto **Jeffrey's Mount**.

An untidy pile of stones marks the otherwise featureless grassy top, from which there is a

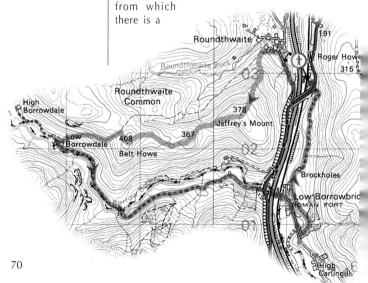

Lune's Bridge

grand view across the foot of Borrowdale to Grayrigg and along the Lune Gorge. Just beyond the summit, swing right, dropping across a dip and then rising over a small mound before descending again and ultimately climbing to Casterfell Hill. The onward trod snakes between the grassy hillocks, gaining height once more towards the more distant top of **Belt Howe** and revealing an impressive picture along Borrowdale as it narrows in its higher reaches below Ashstead Fell. From the top of Belt Howe, the path swings right in descent, passing an isolated boulder and dropping to the base of a shallow dip, where it meets the bridlepath from Roundthwaite.

Looking up Borrowdale to Ashstead Fell

Follow the bridlepath left, quickly giving up height as it wanders into Borrowdale. The way develops as a track that eventually leads to a gate in the intake wall. Continuing down beside the wall, pass through a second gate into the lower pastures, finally coming out at the bottom behind **Low Borrowdale Farm**. Wind around the buildings and through the yard to leave along a track down the valley. After meandering across lush pastures, it crosses a **bridge** and takes a higher line through open woodland of alder, pine, oak, birch and hawthorn. Beyond a gate, pass through a small parking area and walk out to the main road.

Go right and then immediately left towards Carlingill, passing beneath the motorway and the railway. As the lane curves past a junction with the old road from Low Borrowbridge, the field on the right is the site of a **Roman camp**. Later reaching a farm, bear left towards Salterthwaite Bridge.

Immediately over the bridge, double back left through a kissing-gate along a path towards Lune's Bridge. Winding through woodland and then at the edge of pasture, the path follows the boulder-strewn river. Beyond the confluence with Borrow Beck, the steep eastern flanks of Jeffrey's Mount command attention ahead, while to the right, terraces footing the abrupt slopes of Tebay Fell mark the course of a more ancient river.

Pass behind **Brockholes** and then leave the bank, skirting around the buildings to meet a track. Follow it left up the valley, eventually returning to the main road by **Lune's Bridge**.

The earliest mention of **Lune's Bridge** ('Lonesbrig') is from 1379, when a three-year grant was given to levy 'pontage' on goods brought from Hornby Priory to pay for its repair. After the Civil War, it was listed among 16 bridges in Westmorland as being in need of repair, for which a rate was levied across the county. On the western side of Lune's Bridge, at the end of the truncated lane, is a memorial to four railway men. They were struck down by a runaway wagon while working on the line during the early hours of 15 February 2004.

WALK 11
Whinfell and Borrowdale

Start Point	Lay-by on A6 near Huck's Bridge, 9 miles (14.5km) north of Kendal (NY 552 038)
Distance	9 miles (14.5km)
Time	4¾hrs
Terrain	Hill trods and tracks, but may be confusing in mist
Height Gain	680m (2231ft)
Maps	Explorer OL7 – English Lakes (South Eastern area)
Refreshments	Nearest facilities at Kendal
Toilets	None
Parking	Lay-by above Huck's Bridge
Note	The route is not recommended for inexperienced walkers in poor visibility, when map and compass are essential.

Unclaimed by either the Lake District or the Yorkshire Dales National Parks, Borrowdale is surely one of the area's ignored treasures, with splendid walking through the solitude of the dale and along the undulating hills that bound it. A simple there-and-back stroll through its heart can be satisfying in its own right, but this route along the broad southern ridge is a pure delight. With captivating distant views, this is a ramble to be savoured and is best saved for when the weather is clear.

Head south up the road to for 250m to a bend and leave sharp left. Immediately through a gate, strike off right on a climbing path that tackles the snout of Ashstead Fell. The stiff pull shortly levels at a small terrace that looks out towards Morecambe Bay and distant

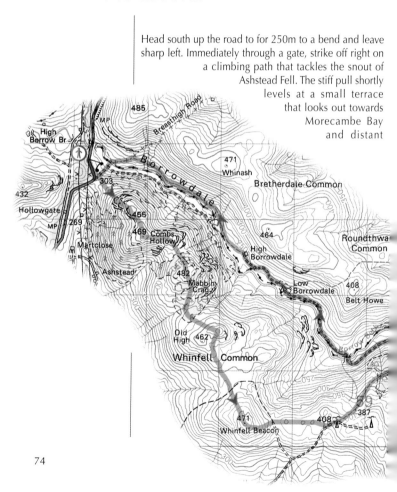

On top of Castle Fell

Blackpool Tower. The path continues less steeply, soon leading to a tall dry-stone cairn, where the panorama sets the tone for the day.

Meandering ahead, a distinct trod links the high points along the broad ridge, embellished by stands of forest and occasional eruptions of gnarled rock. After cresting a height above **Combs Hollow**, which reveals a wonderful view along the valley past Low Borrowdale Farm, the path clambers down towards a saddle. Cross a broken wall and climb along a fire break between conifers to the next top, marked by a ragged pile of stones.

The transmitter masts marking the far end of the ridge now appear beyond the intermediate tops of Castle Fell and Whinfell Beacon as the path descends towards a forested saddle. Reaching a ruined hut at the edge of the plantation, ignore the narrow path delving into thick of the trees and instead go right to find a broader path. Emerging below the trees, clamber over a fence-stile and continue to a ladder-stile at the corner of a wall. The main path stays beside the

387
Birk
Knott

75

wall over Old High, but a short way along branch left on a fainter trod to the higher twin tops of **Castle Fell**, which offer a superb vantage over the valley.

Rejoin the wall path and follow it through a gate into another dip. Beyond a second gate, climb onto **Whinfell Beacon**, its top crossed by a wall and marked by a tall cairn and dilapidated windbreak. The stones are said to have come from a beacon tower that once stood here. It was well sited, for there are grand views to the Howgills, North Pennines, the Lakeland hills and Morecambe Bay.

The way now descends east towards the two radio masts. After crossing a ladder-stile and, later, another intervening wall, the trod ultimately ends at a tarmac track rising from Patton Bridge. Turn up past the first **tower**, but as the track then swings right, branch off left along a path. Keep right at an immediate indistinct fork, briefly paralleling the track before curving above a shallow fold. Becoming clearer, the path loses height to a gate, continuing beyond towards a sparse **woodland** of wind-battered pine. Eventually reach a wall and follow it down to a rough trail, which in turn drops to the main track through the valley.

The valley becomes more rugged above High Borrowdale

Go left, shortly crossing Borrow Beck and later reaching **Low Borrowdale Farm**. Walk through the yard past the house, leaving by a gate in the corner. At first the path tags the slope of the hill, but after a gate falls to the edge of the flood meadows, passing the buildings of **High Borrowdale**, which are sheltered by a clump of trees.

Keep going through occasional gates, eventually reaching a **bridge** across the stream. The track on the southern bank takes you uneventfully back to the road, but a rough trod on this side undulates across the slope of the hill, squeezing the final views from the day.

Walk ahead, passing through a high deer gate and picking your way above grassy tongues that fall to the river. Eventually encounter Breasthigh Road, a rough track dropping from the hills, and follow it down to the river, where massive **stepping-stones** have been set across the beck. Head back up to the main road.

THE WHINFELL

There is more than one Whinfell in Cumbria, and one of them gave its name to a clipper built at Workington in 1861, which spent much of its early life plying the China tea trade between London and Foochow. Sadly its first master, Captain Yeo, died during the ship's second voyage while en route to Sydney, the mate being promoted in his place.

Some 10 years later the ship was sold on, the new owners employing it to transport nitrate from South America. She left Antofagasta in May 1881 on what was to be her final voyage, foundering in heavy weather when only 23 days out. Efforts to save the vessel proved fruitless and the crew finally took to the boats, but by the time they were picked up the next day, one had capsized with the loss of two men. At the resultant naval enquiry held in Valparaiso, the captain and crew were exonerated of any negligence and commended for their diligence in attempting to save the ship.

WALK 12
Carlin Gill

Start Point	Carlingill Bridge (SD 626 996)
Distance	3¼ miles (5.2km)
Time	1½hrs
Terrain	Rough path, which may be impassable after heavy rain
Height Gain	245m (804ft)
Maps	Explorer OL19 – Howgill Fells and Upper Eden Valley
Refreshments	None
Toilets	None
Parking	Roadside parking south of Carlingill Bridge

Carlin Gill offers one of the most dramatic routes within the Howgill Fells and is something not to be missed. The winding valley cleaves deep into the central massif of the hills, creating an air of remoteness almost from the very start. Becoming increasingly rugged, it is a sharp contrast to the rounded grassy slopes above and leads to an impressive waterfall at its head. As the onward ascent into the higher glens demands an awkward scramble, this walk simply turns around and follows the stream back to the lane.

The narrow lane along the main valley high above the Lune follows the course of a Roman road known as the **Western Way**. It linked Ribchester, a strategic crossing point of the River Ribble, to Hadrian's Wall at Carlisle, which defined the northern boundary of the Roman Empire. One of the minor forts along its route lay just 1 mile (1.6km) up the valley at Low Borrowbridge, although little remains visible today.

Carlin Gill defined a stretch of the former boundary between Westmorland and Yorkshire, and Gibbet Hill, which overlooks the gill, was the site of a gallows. Drovers and pack-trains used to travel this lonely route, and cattle thieves and highwaymen were among those hanged there, and perhaps left to rot on the gibbet as a warning to others.

Turn off the lane immediately south of **Carlingill Bridge**, following a path up beside the stream into a narrowing fold. Before long, the valley bends, forcing walkers across the stones in the streambed onto the opposite bank. Soon after, the encroaching slopes step back to receive streams draining Blease Fell and Uldale Head. Ford the side-beck and carry on, the closing walls ushering you into the heart of the mountains. Further up on the right is Haskaw Gill, and then a more spectacular valley down which Small Gill tumbles. Eventually, the path is squeezed out of the ravine's base, picking its way across the steep flanking scree on the left.

Surprisingly the cleft below is well wooded, the precipitous sides giving protection from both the elements and the incessant nibbling of sheep. Carry on past **Black Force**, a boisterous stream well deserving of its name, which cascades from a dark gully that reaches back to the unseen flanks of Fell Head. Beyond the narrowing, the path drops back to the stream, periodically swapping sides to pick the best way to the base of **The Spout**, a 10m fall that blocks the head of the gorge.

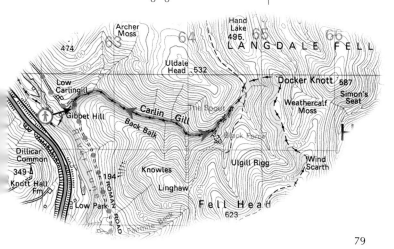

The foot of Black Force

After admiring the spectacle, turn around and head back down the valley to the lane at the start of the route.

WALK 13
Beck Foot

Start Point	Beck Foot (SD 616 965)
Distance	5 miles (8km)
Time	2½hrs
Terrain	Field paths and tracks
Height Gain	280m (918ft)
Maps	Explorer OL19 – Howgill Fells and Upper Eden Valley
Refreshments	Nearest facilities at Sedbergh
Toilets	Sedbergh
Parking	Roadside parking at Beck Foot

Having followed the Lune Gorge for some 5½ miles (8.9km) south from Tebay, both the motorway and West Coast mainline leave the valley to wend their separate ways to Lancaster. Today the ongoing dale carries only minor lanes as it meanders on in the shadow of the Howgills, although until the middle of the last century it too had a railway. Nevertheless, the valley remains a popular passage, since the Dales Way meets the River Lune at the 16th-century Crook of Lune Bridge and follows it down to Sedbergh. It is a very pretty section of the river and one of the highlights of the long-distance trail. The route can readily be combined with Walk 14 to make a satisfying full-day's expedition.

At **Beck Foot** begin opposite the Lowgill Viaduct along a lane signed to Beck Foot, Lambrigg and Killington. Take the first left, crossing a stream to climb away beyond Half Island House along an old hollow way. Reaching a junction, go left, the track still rising to reveal inspiring views to the Howgills and the Whinfell ridge.

The 30m-high **Lowgill Viaduct**, dominating the tiny settlement, opened in 1860 to carry the Ingleton Railway to its junction with the Lancaster–Carlisle line, just to the north. The railway ran from Ingleton to Kirkby Lonsdale and then followed the Lune past Sedbergh to Lowgill. It had been intended as a main route from London via Leeds to Carlisle and Scotland, but the politics of rival companies left the line in two halves at Ingleton. By the time the connection was made, the initiative had been lost and the main traffic adopted the Settle–Carlisle route. Yet, the Ingleton Railway enjoyed a brief moment of glory before the track was finally taken up, when extraordinary snowfall blocked the summit section of its rival during the winter of 1962–3. For a few weeks until the thaw, the London–Scotland express was diverted along the Ingleton line.

Beyond the Lowgill Viaduct towards Fell Head

Meeting the corner of a track at the top, go left through **High House Farm**, resuming your ascent beyond to a

gate. The onward path lies through another gate, ahead, but briefly deviate left to steal a glimpse back to the Lune Valley.

Through the gate, walk on beside the left wall from field to field, the rise cresting to reveal a wonderful panorama of the Lake District. Descend to a dip, and cross a slatted bridge and then a stile to continue on the opposite flank of the wall. Emerging onto a **lane**, go left for ½ mile (800m) over Hilltop Heights. Middleton Fell and Cragg Hill now come into sight, with Whernside behind. Some 300m beyond the summit leave through a field gate on the left, from which a signed trod heads towards the valley. Over a stile, continue on a contained path down to **Hill Top Farm**. Walk through the yard to leave by a gate at the bottom. Drop across a final field to a lane at Goodies.

The graceful Crook of Lune Bridge was built in the 16th century

Turn right past a cottage and then swing left through a field gate beside the entrance drive to a second house. Walk past the corner of a derelict barn and head straight down into the valley. Cross the course of the **Ingleton Railway** and continue to a **footbridge** spanning the River Lune.

On the far bank, the path briefly heads upstream before turning alongside Smithy Beck to a junction with the Dales Way. Crossing the stream, walk back to continue north beside the river, which here is narrow and hurries over a rocky bed. The way meanders on pleasantly for a good mile (1.6km), crossing Chapel Beck and eventually entering **Crook of Lune Wood**. Towards its far end, watch for a sign nudging the path from the bank to leave the trees through a gate. Head across an open pasture, short-cutting a sharp bend of the river. It is one of two stretches known as the Crook of Lune – the other lies a little way above Lancaster. Emerging onto a lane walk downhill to the elegant two-arched **Crook of Lune Bridge**.

Immediately over the bridge, turn through a gate on the right. Follow a grass track into the next field and continue beside the left hedge. Higher up, move towards the crumbling foundations of Nether House, from which an old green track leads up to a gate and narrow lane. The way lies to the left, swinging over a **bridge** that spanned the former railway. Around a second bend in front of the West Coast line, descend past Lowgill Farm to the **B6257**. **Beck Foot** is just to the left.

WALK 14
Firbank and Bridge End

Start Point	Goodies, Firbank, B6257 1½ miles (2.4km) north of the A684 (SD 625 943)
Distance	5 miles (8km)
Time	2½hrs
Terrain	Field paths and tracks
Height Gain	290m (951ft)
Maps	Explorer OL19 – Howgill Fells and Upper Eden Valley
Refreshments	Nearest facilities at Sedbergh
Toilets	Sedbergh
Parking	Limited roadside parking at Goodies
Note	If flooded, the ford at Crosdale Beck can be avoided by a short detour.

After meandering through the pastures footing the Howgills, this route climbs to the higher ground on the western side of the valley, from where there are superb views to Brant Fell. Notable features along the way include an impressive viaduct, built to take the Ingleton Railway across the Lune, and Fox's Pulpit, a lonely crag high above Firbank, where George Fox preached an open-air sermon to a congregation of over 1000 people in June 1652.

A footpath leaves the lane just south of **Goodies** through a field gate beside the entrance to a cottage. Walk past the corner of a derelict barn and head down beside the

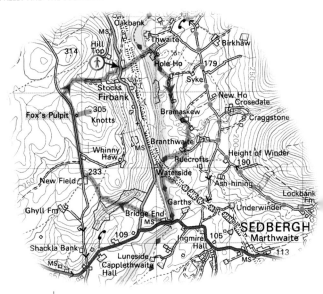

hedge into the valley. Cross the trackbed of the **old railway** and continue to a **footbridge** spanning the river.
On the far bank, follow the contained path left and then
right, climbing beside Smithy Beck to a junction with the
Dales Way.

Turn right beneath an archway to **Hole House Farm**
and walk through the yards. From a gate beyond, the
Dales Way towards Nether Bainbridge is signed over
the rise of the hill, where a superb view opens along the
valley. The course of the former Ingleton Railway can be
seen on the opposite side, running north to an impressive viaduct over which it linked to the Lancaster–Carlisle
route at Lowgill. To the east, the ground rises steeply to
Arrant Haw, with Calders and The Calf behind.

Of the two adjacent gates at the far side of the field,
go through the one on the right and stride on by the left
wall to Nether Bainbridge. At a three-way sign in the corner by the farm, go right past the side of a barn, then

pass through a gated squeeze-stile to follow a track to the right. At the end, continue through a gated pen and keep going at the field edge. Further on, pass left of an isolated length of wall and then dogleg in front of a small barn. A trod guides you on across the pasture, gently curving left up to a ladder-stile at a wall corner. Carry on by the left boundary to the farm at **Bramaskew**.

A mason's mark on one of the stones of the Lune Viaduct

Mount a stile behind the farm and walk straight out to the top field corner. The Dales Way continues through a wooden gate as a contained path. Breaking out at the field edge, carry on downhill to a ladder-stile near a barn at **Low Branthwaite**. Walk on, crossing a track to another stile beside a field gate and keep ahead at the field edge above the deepening trough of Crosdale Beck. Over a stile, bear right from the gully on a trod leading down to the base of the Lune Viaduct. As you pass by, notice that some of the massive stones bear masons' marks, which identified their work for payment. Continuing downstream it is then necessary to ford **Crosdale Beck**.

Unless there has been heavy rain, it should be possible to cross without water overlapping your boots.

The River Lune above Lincoln's Inn Bridge

Otherwise, retrace your steps to Low Branthwaite Farm and go right along its track. Once over the bridge, leave to follow the beck above its southern bank, crossing the intervening embankment to return to the Lune.

Beyond the stream and over a stile, accompany the main river at the edge of successive fields to the A684 beside **Lincoln's Inn Bridge**. Cross the river, but leave the road some 30m beyond Lincoln's Inn Bridge Farm over a stile on the right. Follow the fence away. Emerging onto a narrow lane, take the gate opposite and head up at the field edge. Bear left beyond the corner to locate a fence-stile into **Hawkrigg Wood**, from which a slanting path rises through the trees. Breaking into a field above, maintain the same line, climbing past the corner of a wire fence to two adjacent gates. Go through the one on the right and strike a right diagonal across more fields to meet a track that leads out to a lane beside **New Field Farm**. Walk uphill for ½ mile (800m) to a small enclosure near the crest.

A kissing-gate beside the graveyard enclosure gives access to the fell and **Fox's Pulpit**, but clamber on over

Fox's Pulpit

the hill behind the rock for a view across the valley that is hard to surpass.

Return to the lane and carry on for another 300m before leaving over a stile on the right. Follow the field edge down the hill, passing through a couple of gates to continue beside a gully wooded with larch, oak, ash and sycamore. The path then moves away to pass through a gate. Walk down a field, watching for a contained track on the left, which winds down to the lane at **Goodies**.

GEORGE FOX AND THE QUAKERS

The walled enclosure is the graveyard of a small chapel that succumbed to a winter storm in 1839, and all but one of the tombstones lie recumbent and overgrown, overshadowed by a small stand of windswept pine. But great things happened here in the summer of 1652.

Like many others of his day, George Fox could not accept the institutionalised ritual of the established church and sought a simpler, egalitarian spirituality. In travelling around the country preaching a doctrine of 'inner light', he attracted a growing following and, having experienced a vision on Pendle Hill of 'many souls coming to Christ', came to Sedbergh and then here, where he preached for three hours to over 1000 people.

That event is seen as the founding moment of the Quaker movement, the Religious Society of Friends, and a plaque has been mounted upon a nearby rock, since known as Fox's Pulpit. It reads

'Let your lives speak.
Here or near this rock George Fox preached
to about one thousand seekers for three
hours on Sunday June 13, 1652. Great power
inspired his message and the meeting proved
of the first importance in gathering the Society
of Friends known as the Quakers. Many men and
women convinced of the truth on this fell and
in other parts of the northern counties went
forth through the land and over the seas with
the living word of the Lord enduring great
hardships and winning multitudes to Christ.'

WALK 15
Winder, Calders and The Calf

Start Point	Sedbergh (SD 657 921)
Distance	9¾ miles (15.7km)
Time	4½hrs
Terrain	Indistinct upland trods; return along a lane
Height Gain	855m (2805ft)
Maps	Explorer OL19 – Howgill Fells and Upper Eden Valley
Refreshments	Pubs and cafés in Sedbergh
Toilets	Beside car parks
Parking	Car parks in Sedbergh (pay and display)
Note	Fording Long Rigg Beck, near the end of the walk, may involve a paddle (no alternative).

The grassy flanks of the Howgills rear as a formidable backdrop to Sedbergh, the peripheral summits serving as stepping-stones to the cluster of higher tops behind. The first pull is the most exacting and leads over Winder and Calders onto The Calf, the highest point of the group of hills. The climb has been a traditional challenge for Sedbergh School's pupils and is immortalised in the refrain of their ancient song,

> '…Tis the hills that are stood around us,
>   unchanged since our days began.
>   It is Cautley, Calf and Winder,
>   that make the Sedbergh man.'

This walk follows the path trodden by countless lads (and now lasses) of the school onto the tops, dropping back over White Fell to return along the more gentle flanks of the Lune Valley.

Begin in **Sedbergh** from the junction of Main Street and Finkle Street, by St Andrew's Church at the western end of the town, and head past the post office in the direction of Kendal. Take the first street off on the right, just past the

Dalesman pub. Follow it up behind the town, winding
above playing fields and past the houses beyond. As they
fizzle out, bear off right on a track signed as a permissive
path up to **Lockbank Farm**.

At the top, walk through a gate to the right of the
building ahead, from which a short track rises to the
open fell. Go left beside the wall,
but almost immediately bear
off right on a path

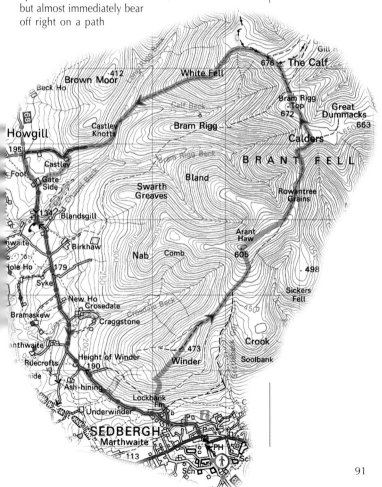

that determinedly attacks the southern flank of **Winder**. Fragmenting higher up, the path offers a choice of routes to the summit, but none escape the steep climb. The compensation, however, is the splendid view opening behind of Middleton Fell, Great Coum, Whernside and Rise Hill, while over to the south-east is the great mass of Baugh Fell. Eventually, the lessening gradient heralds the approaching top, and the concrete trig column suddenly springs into view. Beside it is a topograph, erected to commemorate the millennium and which helps identify the surrounding hills visible from this superb vantage.

The onward path runs ahead in gradual descent along the north-eastern rib of the hill, falling to meet a lower path from Lockbank Farm that has bypassed the summit. Beyond a shallow saddle, take the left fork and climb on towards **Arant Haw**. After another stiff pull, the ground abruptly levels, but, despite the significantly greater altitude, there is no trig column, just a melancholy pile of pebbles that has more the appearance of an abandoned campfire hearth than a cairn.

Bear right along a broad grassy shoulder, the great sweeping ridges that buttress the western flanks of

The melancholy pile of pebbles on Arant Haw

the Howgills presenting a dramatic sight. Unhurriedly descend to rejoin the path that contoured the south-eastern slope and continue over **Rowantree Grains**, where yawning gullies bite deep into the hill from both sides. Beyond, the pace settles once more into a steady plod up the steepening southern ridge of **Calders**. The top is marked by a pile of stones, notable only because of the lack of any obvious source of building material. With all the strenuous work now behind you, turn left and enjoy the undulating ½ mile (800m) stroll over the intermediate **Bram Rigg Top** onto **The Calf**.

From the top of The Calf

There is remarkable consistency in the heights of the main Howgill summits, and **The Calf** only manages a bare 2m supremacy over Calders. It is, however, graced by a trig column, and just to the side in a shallow scrape is a small tarn. The views are truly magnificent, and reach out west to the distant jagged peaks of Lakeland and around Morecambe Bay to the shimmering Celtic sea. Turning around to the east brings in Baugh Fell and Wild Boar Fell, while behind, the long spine of watershed hills stretches north past High Seat to far-off Nine Standards Rigg.

93

Continue past the trig, but then bear left off the main path, making for the lower, flat-topped outrider of White Fell Head. Over to the right, the eye is drawn into the head of Langdale, which slices north through the hills for almost 6 miles (9.7km) to meet the infant River Lune. At a later fork, keep left, curving around the southern edge of the plateau to begin a descent along the drawn-out tongue of **White Fell**. As the gradient steepens, there is an impressive view across the deep fold of Calf Beck, the ground falling to the confluence of streams in the intimacy of the valley below.

A developing track drops to a stony ford across Long Rigg Beck, which, after rain, can be something of a paddle. As the way rounds the apron of **Castley Knotts**, pause to glance back at the superb setting of the upper valley, for all too suddenly the track turns from the fell between the confining walls of the lower enclosures. Reaching a junction above **Castley Farm**, there is a choice. Either bear right and follow the track out to Four Lane Ends, or alternatively cut across the fields to Gate Side – both routes lead out to Howgill Lane.

If opting for the fields, turn down towards the farm and then swing right past the end of the farmhouse to go through the right-most of two gates into the field behind. Walk away beside the right-hand fence and across the top corner of the field beyond to encounter a sign to Gate Side. Bear right to a ladder-stile and then keep ahead, dipping to cross a stream. A grass track leads to the lower of two gates, which is passed through to skirt below farm buildings to a final ladder-stile.

For both routes, after emerging onto Howgill Lane, go left, following it down to a bridge across **Chapel Beck**, the stream forded earlier. Through a gate over to the right is the tiny church of Holy Trinity, set within a pretty graveyard shaded by neatly trimmed yews. The way back, however, lies with the main lane. After a mile (1.6km), branch left at a fork, picking up the outward route at **Lockbank** to return to **Sedbergh**.

WALK 16

Sedbergh and the River Rawthey

Start Point	Sedbergh (SD 657 921)
Distance	5 miles (8km)
Time	2¼hrs
Terrain	Field paths and trods
Height Gain	145m (477ft)
Maps	Explorer OL19 – Howgill Fells and Upper Eden Valley
Refreshments	Pubs and cafés in Sedbergh
Toilets	Beside car parks
Parking	Car parks in Sedbergh (pay and display)

Above Sedbergh, the narrowing valley of the River Rawthey becomes squeezed between the soaring Howgills and the lower slopes of Rise Hill and Baugh Fell. This undemanding ramble begins along the Howgills' lower slopes, passing the castle that oversaw the early development of Sedbergh, and returns beside the river by the ruin of another lookout, a folly dating from the 19th century.

From the junction by St Andrew's Church in **Sedbergh**, walk along Main Street through the centre of town. Meeting Long Lane at the end, go left and immediately left again before Westwood Books up a track towards Castlehaw. As the route breaks from the trees above the town, the mound of Castlehaw comes into view across to the right. The access is over a stile as the track shortly curves right.

An early Norman stronghold dating from the end of the 11th century, the **castle** held a commanding position above the entrance to the Rawthey valley. Exploiting a small outcrop, the steep-sided motte, on which stood a defensible wooden tower, still

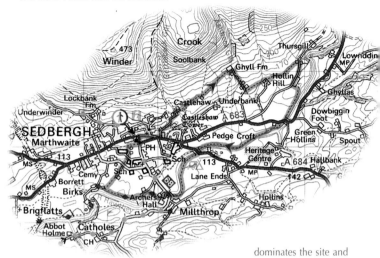

dominates the site and would have been further defended by a deep ditch and wooden palisade. The living area lay within the bailey, the lower apron projecting to the west, and contained the lord's hall as well as quarters for his retainers and dependants. With the consolidation of Norman rule, it became redundant and was never rebuilt in stone, as were those further to the north. It was, however, brought back into use during the last war as a lookout for the Royal Observer Corps.

Return to the track and continue to **Castlehaw Farm**, swinging left in front of the barns and then right across a stream past Howgills Bunk Barn. Through a gate, walk ahead across the fields beyond, contouring above the bottom fence to an isolated barn. Keep going, later crossing a couple of ladder-stiles to find the boundary now on your left. Bounded by the abruptly rising slopes of the Howgills, the views are captivating. Ahead, the great rounded hump of Baugh Fell falls to the foot of Garsdale, while to the right Frostrow Fells prelude the higher ground of Aye Gill Pike.

The onward path to Ghyll Farm

The River Rawthey below Straight Bridge

Reaching **Ghyll Farm**, exit to the right of the barns and follow its track away. At a fork, just beyond a cattle-grid, bear left into Stone Hill Farm, looking for a small white gate on the right into the cobbled yard fronting the house. Leave through a field gate at the bottom and walk left at the field edge past the barns. Over a footbridge, continue to the next farm, **Hollin Hill**.

Bear left past the farmhouse and through the yard to the fields beyond. Carry on across the hillside, over a stile and past the end of a truncated wall to find another stile just above a white house. Walk down to emerge beside it onto Buckbank Lane. Turn right to Buckbank Farm and enter the yard. Go right between the barns and then left beside the silage store to the field. Follow the perimeter down and continue above the wooded ravine of the River Rawthey to meet the main road at Straight Bridge.

The way continues, through a gap stile opposite, beside the river to the **A684** at New Bridge. Over the Rawthey, turn through a kissing-gate and carry on down-stream, emerging by another bridge at **Millthrop**. Cross back to find a gated stile, just beyond a drive. Strike out above the mill, briefly rejoining the river to enter a small wood. Watch for the waymarked path swinging right between sunken walls, at the end of which, walk forward and take the right-most of the forking paths to a gate at the edge of the trees. Go left and carry on beyond the corner of the wood and the ruin of an octagonal tower.

Known as the **Pepper Pot** and dating from the end of the 19th century, the tower was a gazebo or summer-house within the gardens of Akay House. The house was demolished just before the Second World War, but the tower, originally rising to two storeys, was left to crumble in its own good time. The folly became the scene of excitement when a cow wandered in, managing to reach the first floor, and an old photo-graph shows it gazing bemusedly from the window.

The path falls from the field to rejoin the river, running past one of Sedbergh School's rugby pitches to a stile. Swing away from the river, heading upfield towards a barn. Emerging onto a track, follow it out to Busk Lane. Through a kissing-gate opposite, climb to another gate at the top of the bank and, crossing a path, continue beside the school cricket pitch. At the end go right, coming out onto Finkle Street in **Sedbergh** beside St Andrew's churchyard.

Low and wide, **St Andrew's** is typical of many of the Dales' churches and seems completely at one with the surrounding countryside. Its most notable feature is the stained glass filling the eastern window, which was installed at the end of the 19th century by one of the town's great benefactors, Mrs Upton-Cottrell-Dormer of Ingmire Hall. In 1906, she presented the town with the Queen's Gardens to commemorate Victoria's long reign, but the window here was given in memory of her husband and parents. Depicting Jesus calling his first disciples, Simon (called Peter) and Andrew to be 'fishers of men', it was designed by Victor Milner, who was considered to be one of the finest craftsmen of his day, and made by Watsons of Baker Street in London.

WALK 17

Frostrow Fells and Dentdale

Start Point	Sedbergh (SD 656 920)
Distance	6¾ miles (10.9km)
Time	3¼hrs
Terrain	Lanes, tracks and moorland trods
Height Gain	295m (962ft)
Maps	Explorer OL19 – Howgill Fells and Upper Eden Valley and Explorer OL2 – Yorkshire Dales (Southern and Western areas)
Refreshments	Sedbergh
Toilets	Sedbergh
Parking	Loftus Hill car park (pay and display)

Today, the road to Dent from Sedbergh follows the river into the dale, but an older track climbs over Frostrow, the low shoulder of Aye Gill Pike. This walk combines the best of both routes and reveals some superb scenery in this gentle corner on the fringe of the Yorkshire Dales.

Looking back across Long Moor to the Howgills

In **Sedbergh**
stride down
Loftus Hill, cross-
ing a bridge over the River
Rawthey at the bottom. Take the
first left into **Millthrop**, going left again in
the village. At **Lane Ends**, turn right along Frostrow
Lane, which eventually leads past **Hollins** to Side Farm. A
rough bridleway continues ahead through a gate onto the
open fell. Walk for 150m, cross a stream and then turn off
right past the grassed mounds of old workings. Pick up a
faint trod that then curves left to parallel the bridleway.
Beyond a confusion of quad tracks, a more distinct path
settles on a south-easterly heading towards **Long Moor
Moss**. After crossing a stream the way eventually leads
to a ladder-stile in a stone wall. Maintain the same direction, steadily diverging from the boundary and heading
towards the angle of a wall in the middle distance. Carry
on past the corner to a gate in the end boundary.

Although not reaching any summit along the way, the path gives a fine **vantage** to the surrounding hills. To the east beyond Garsdale is Baugh Fell, a great lump of a hill whose streams all find their way into the River Lune, while overlooking Dentdale are Middleton Fell and Crag Hill. Crag Hill's abrupt northern face was dug for both coal and stone, and halfway up the slope are the famous Meggar Stones, a group of tall cairns raised by the quarrymen.

Helmside is signed to the right through a second gate. The way drops at the edge of marginal pasture towards the Dent valley. Lower down, move from the wall towards a gate in the bottom boundary, from which a shepherd's track guides you towards the farm. Through a gate, the track swings left, but keep ahead, passing right of barns. Go over a stile and along a track into the yard, walking between the buildings to the lane beyond.

To the right, stride out along the lane for ½ mile (800m), passing **Mire House** to reach Craggs Farm. Leave through a gate on the right, the way signed to Millthrop. Follow the wall away to a squeeze-stile and strike upfield to Leakses Farm. Over a stile, climb the steps opposite to a small yard in front of the farmhouse. Wind left through the yard, but where the track then swings left, keep ahead between a barn and shed into the field behind. Head from field to field towards **Burton Hill Farm**, which shortly appears.

Exit the field beside barns over a ladder-stile onto a track. Walk through the yard and past the farmhouse, leaving through a metal gate in the far right corner. Keep with the bottom boundary into the next field, but then, part-way along, bear right to **Hewthwaite**, which then comes into sight.

Leave through gates onto a crossing track and, taking the stile opposite, keep going to **Gap Farm**. Joining its access, walk right and then bear left on a grass track past the front of the farmhouse. Head across the field towards **Gap Wood**, passing through a gate to continue along a walled track at its fringe.

Where the track subsequently forks at a waymark, bear right, curving out of Dentdale over the shoulder of the hill. Through a gate, the track winds across access land before dropping off the fell into **Millthrop**. Go right through the village, turning left and then right onto the main road. Follow it back over the bridge up into **Sedbergh**.

At the edge of Gap Wood

WALK 18

Beside the River Dee from Dent

Start Point	Dent (SD 704 871)
Distance	6 miles (9.7km)
Time	2½hrs
Terrain	Lanes and field paths
Height Gain	130m (427ft)
Maps	Explorer OL2 – Yorkshire Dales (Southern and Western areas)
Refreshments	Dent
Toilets	Dent
Parking	Car park in Dent (pay and display)

Although most dales in the area take the name from the river flowing through them, Dentdale is an exception. Its river is the Dee, which has its source high up on Blea Moor and joins the Rawthey below Sedbergh to flow into the Lune. Dentdale is justifiably proclaimed as the prettiest of the dales, and the village at its heart is not to be missed. This wander downriver through the meadows and return on the northern bank, largely along quiet lanes, enables a leisurely appreciation of the valley's undoubted charms.

From the car park in **Dent**, follow the main street into the village. Keep left at successive junctions, passing the granite fountain to the memory of the Victorian geologist Adam Sedgwick and then the church, set back from the road, to eventually meet the river at the 18th-century **Church Bridge**. Leave through a squeeze-stile immediately before it and head downstream at the edge of successive meadows. After ½ mile (800m), slip briefly onto the lane before rejoining the riverside path through a kissing-gate towards Barth Bridge.

Cross the lane at **Barth Bridge** and continue beside the river, the way now signed to Ellers. After a mile (1.6km), passing below the farm at **Dillicar**, watch for a waymark directing you out to the lane. Go right, soon reaching a **footbridge** across the Dee. Walk left above the northern bank, but after the second stile drop from the embankment into the adjacent field. Head to a gate in the corner and then bear left towards Low Mire House Farm. Exit the far corner of the field, cross a stream and follow a track to the lane opposite **Mire House**.

Go right for ½ mile (800m). Beyond the Dent Crafts tea room, turn in at the entrance to **Helmside Farm** by a sign to Rawridding. Walk past the farmhouse and turn right through a gate. Climb away on a concrete track, but where it bends right, keep ahead through a gate on a field track. Through another gate in the top corner, keep by the left wall, crossing a couple of stiles and passing a lime kiln built into the boundary.

Keep with the wall to leave by a gate tucked in the corner, from which a grass track leads to **Rawridding**. Go past the front of the farmhouse and down its drive to meet a narrow lane. Turn uphill, taking the right fork towards **Hining Farm**. At the end of the hedge, negotiate a squeeze-stile on the right and walk downfield, looking for a gated stile breaking the left boundary. An old track runs down past

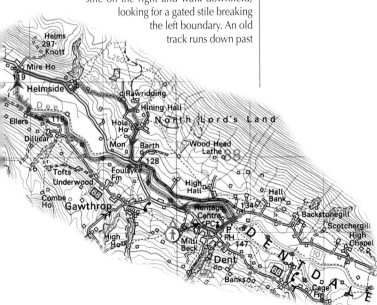

Cobbled streets give Dent an air of timelessness

a farm to another lane. Follow it downhill to the main dale lane and head left to **Barth Bridge**.

Turn off immediately before the bridge along a narrow lane hugging the riverbank. Later moving away, it continues between flower-rich hedges, through which, opposite Low Hall, there is a fine picture to Dent and its church. A little further on, look for a stile in the right hedge. Cross to the river and follow it upstream to **Church Bridge**. Climb out to the lane and return to **Dent**.

106

WALK 19
Killington

Start Point	Killington New Bridge on B6256 (SD 622 908)
Distance	6½ miles (10.5km)
Time	3hrs
Terrain	Field paths, tracks and lanes
Height Gain	280m (919ft)
Maps	Explorer OL2 – Yorkshire Dales (Southern and Western areas) and Explorer OL19 – Howgill Fells and Upper Eden Valley
Refreshments	None
Toilets	None
Parking	Roadside parking east of Killington New Bridge

Killington is known for its motorway service area and the lake that lies below it, a reservoir completed in 1819 to supply the Lancaster Canal and now a noted haunt for fishermen. The tiny village from which they both take their name lies a couple of miles away on the other side of the hill, but is a world apart, set in a landscape of gently rolling hills and looking out across the Lune Valley to the Howgills and western Dales. It is the focus of this pleasant countryside walk, which begins from a small nature reserve. After briefly following the River Lune, the ramble rises onto the higher ground of Park Hill, from where there are superb views to the Howgills and Middleton Fell.

The stretch of Lune just above its confluence with the River Rawthey below Sedbergh is little visited but particularly beautiful, and a short wander north along the nature path on the eastern side of the river is a fine prelude to the main walk. The steep bank is well wooded, but there are views to the water where salmon can sometimes be seen leaping.

Cross the road bridge and take the first turning on the left towards Killington and Old Hutton. Initially the quiet lane runs only within earshot of the river, but then closes above a shallow gorge where the water tumbles over a rocky bed of grey slate. At the end of a crash barrier, cross a low ladder-stile and continue along the tree-lined bank. Passing a hut beside a **weir**, the path turns through the yard of the converted Kingfisher Mill. Instead of leaving along its drive, keep ahead past a shed at the edge of a lawned garden to rejoin the riverside.

Later emerge onto a track and go left to the farms at **Stangerthwaite**. Swing right and wind on between flower-rich hedgerows, eventually reaching a junction of lanes. Take that to the left, walking for ½ mile (800m) to **Hallbeck**. Stay with the lane across the bridge, but then turn off beside a cottage along an old path signed to Aikrigg. Beyond the end of a wall, the path curves alongside an outgrown hedge to run above Hall Beck. In due course, over a couple of stiles, the path climbs from the stream to a junction.

The path to the right offers a short-cut to Killington, but the main route lies in the other direction. Views open across the valley to Middleton Fell as the ancient way slopes across the hillside, shortly dropping to cottages at **Beckside**. Turn right over a bridge and go right again before the entrance to Beckside Farm, the way signed to Harprigg. Just 20m up the track, turn off left over a stile to follow a narrow trackway rising at the field edge. As it opens out, keep beside the hedge, but then, passing through a

The River Lune above Kingfisher Mill

108

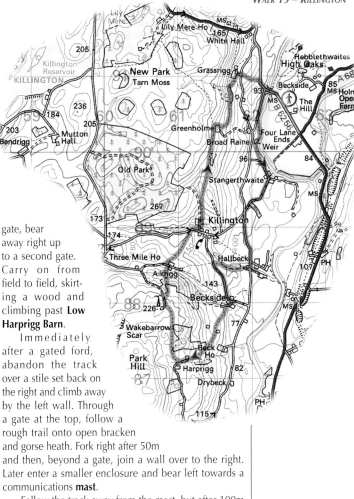

gate, bear away right up to a second gate. Carry on from field to field, skirting a wood and climbing past **Low Harprigg Barn**.

Immediately after a gated ford, abandon the track over a stile set back on the right and climb away by the left wall. Through a gate at the top, follow a rough trail onto open bracken and gorse heath. Fork right after 50m and then, beyond a gate, join a wall over to the right. Later enter a smaller enclosure and bear left towards a communications **mast**.

Follow the track away from the mast, but after 100m leave through a gate on the right. Bear left, dropping to a fence-stile near the end of a wall. Aim half-left again, picking up a grass track that soon descends through trees to a gate and stream at the foot of the hill. Over a footbridge just to the right, join the track up to **Aikrigg**.

Take the field track through a gate beside the barn opposite. Keep right at a fork and then, a little further on, slip through a hedge gap to continue on its other flank. Later, over a ladder-stile, carry on to the bottom field corner, there emerging onto a narrow lane above **Killington**. Walk down to the hamlet and take the first left, which leads past the church and Killington Hall.

KILLINGTON HALL

The original moated hall at Killington was established by William de Pickering, who acquired the manor around 1260 in return for the yearly service of a pair of gilt spurs to the barony of Kendale. His descendants strengthened its defence with a three-storey crenellated pele tower and remained there until the line died out in 1582.

The ruined tower stands beside a more comfortable manor house built in the 17th century, which carries above the doorway the crest of the Uptons of Ingmire, who arrived during the 19th century. The Pickering arms can be seen in a fragment of medieval glass incorporated within one of northern windows in the church opposite.

Dedicated to All Saints, the church is probably the original family chapel and contemporary with the 14th-century pele tower. After Henry VIII's break with Rome the family retained Catholic sympathies, and there was supposedly a priest's hole within the house and a secret underground passage connecting to the church.

Carry on to the end of the track, turning right in front of Lockwood Cottage over a stream into a field. Climb left to a narrow gate in the corner and keep going above the stream at the edge of two more fields. Passing through another gate, strike for the top of the hill. Walk on above Lammas Plantation to find a track that gently loses height beside a wall towards **Greenholme Farm**. Before reaching it, however, branch off left over a stile to contour above the farm. Pass into a second field and then drop right on a rough track into the farmyard.

The oldest parts of Killington Hall date back to the 13th century

Leaving the yard, turn sharp left through a gate into the corner of a field. Stay with the top boundary to a second gate and continue across the slope of the hill into Cowby Wood. As the trees thin at the far side, the path falls to adjacent gates and stiles in the bottom corner. Hop over the stile on the right and turn left across a stream. Keep ahead to **Grassrigg Farm**, leaving the field to follow its track right up to a lane. Take the gate opposite and head straight out to a second gate. Maintain the same line, descending past a solitary oak to meet the **B6256** and go right back to New Killington Bridge.

WALK 20
Calf Top

Start Point	Barbon (SD 628 823)
Distance	8¼ miles (13.3km)
Time	5¼hrs
Terrain	Hill paths
Height Gain	665m (2182ft)
Maps	Explorer OL2 – Yorkshire Dales (Southern and Western areas)
Refreshments	Barbon Inn
Toilets	None
Parking	Car park by village hall

Although the boundary of the Yorkshire Dales National Park climbs to the crest of Middleton Fell, the bulk of the hill is excluded from its confines. This in no way detracts from its gentle beauty as this walk reveals, which climbs from Barbon to Calf Top, the fell's highest point, and then wanders west to a prominent 'stone man' for the views across the Lune Valley. Although the ongoing path descends to the edge of the access land at Mill House, there is no legitimate link to the footpath there, and the return, therefore, is by the outward route.

BARBONDALE

Middleton Fell is sliced from the main body of the Dales by the steep-sided valley of Barbondale, part of the Dent Fault that runs between Kirkby Stephen and Kirkby Lonsdale. Like the Howgills to the north, its geological affinity is to the west, where long, fragmented grassy tongues fall to the Lune Valley, a stark contrast to the sheer abruptness with which its other flank plummets into Barbondale.

Barbon's importance increased during the 19th century with the construction of the railway that linked the settlements on the western fringe of the Dales, and the church was built to cater for the growing population. But the spate was short-lived and, now bypassed too by the main road, the village again finds itself off the beaten track. Rural quiet pervades except during three weekends a year, when it is the venue for the Barbon Speed Hill Climb – an exciting event for motor enthusiasts, but best avoided by those seeking solitude.

Leaving the car park, go left into **Barbon**. Turn right by the war memorial, passing the Barbon Inn. Just beyond the church, go left and follow the drive over the beck. After bending right, swing left off the track and head out across the park. Skirting the top of Ellers Wood, pass through a gate and keep going to **Eskholme**. Behind the farm, veer right, climbing along an old boundary to a gate in the intake wall. A quad track strikes a circuitous course up the hill, endeavouring to lessen the gradient around the craggy buttress of **Eskholme Pike**. A cairn marks the highpoint of the limestone outcrop, the detour to which is rewarded by a commanding panorama.

A clear trod continues to the east, the gradient now easier along the broad snout of the hill. Although the steady plod later steepens, the view is all-distracting, with Barbon Low Fell

Middleton Fell

592

Calf Top 610

Calf

Barkin

232

Cattle Grid

Howegill Head

219

203

Castle Knott 536

Barbondale

Borwens
Barwick Hall
Thorn Moor

Eskholme Pike 307 Cairn

Eskholme

Barbon Park

Barbon Manor

169 175

bon

End

PH

124

Underfell

Low Bank Ho 343

113

The detour to the tiny cairn atop Eskholme Pike is rewarded with a splendid view

and Crag Hill the immediate neighbours. Keep going past a small pile of stones, with the path curving beyond and in time reaching the cairn on **Castle Knott**.

Beyond the cairn, the way falls to a shallow saddle before climbing once more to the main bulk of the hill. Out to the north-west is an isolated pillar, the 'stone man' to be visited a little later in the walk. Eventually reach the corner of a wall and keep uphill beside it, the white survey column on the summit of **Calf Top** soon coming into view.

The vista from **Calf Top** is grand, a panoramic sweep across Yorkshire, Cumbria and Lancashire. To the north, the ground erupts spectacularly in the steeply buttressed Howgills, while to the left, keen eyes might spot Shap Fell, Helvellyn, Scafell, The Old Man of Coniston and Black Combe. To the east are Baugh Fell, Aye Gill Pike and, behind them, Wild Boar Fell, with Great Knoutberry Hill, Great Shunner and Lovely Seat further round. Across the deep rift of Barbondale are Great Coum and Gragareth, and although the summit of Whernside is masked by the intervening Great Coum, Ingleborough is there for all to see.

A faint trod strikes left from the trig column across the heather, shortly joining a shepherd's track that winds past a shallow pool. Keep going to reach the **'stone man' pillar** spied earlier, a substantial dry-stone tower rising beside the path.

> Such **cairns** are generously scattered around these northern hills, the most famous, perhaps, are those on Gragareth, Wild Boar Fell and of course Nine Standards Rigg. Their age and purpose has often been lost in time and some have become enmeshed in legend. Credible theories suggest boundary markers or waypoints, but many were probably built by quarrymen or shepherds working on the lonely moors. Like the one here, they are invariably well made and stand as notable features in an otherwise empty landscape.

The path continues invitingly in a long, pleasurable descent for another 1¾ miles (2.8km) to the bottom of the hill by Mill House, but 10m of private track separates the access boundary from the footpath. So, having taken your fill of the view out to the west, head back to the survey pillar on **Calf Top** and follow your outward route back to **Barbon**.

Looking across the head of Barbondale to distant Great Knoutberry Hill

WALK 21
Barbon Low Fell

Start Point	Barbon (SD 628 823)
Distance	8½ miles (13.7km)
Time	4¼hrs
Terrain	Hill paths
Height Gain	420m (1378ft)
Maps	Explorer OL2 – Yorkshire Dales (Southern and Western areas)
Refreshments	Barbon Inn
Toilets	None
Parking	Car park by village hall

Barbon Low Fell overlooks the foot of Barbondale, and forces a turn in the lively beck that runs through the dale to the River Lune. This circuit around the flanks of the hill leaves the deep valley to give a taste of the higher moors, but soon turns to drop back along old forgotten lanes.

Sheep crossing the ford of Barbon Beck

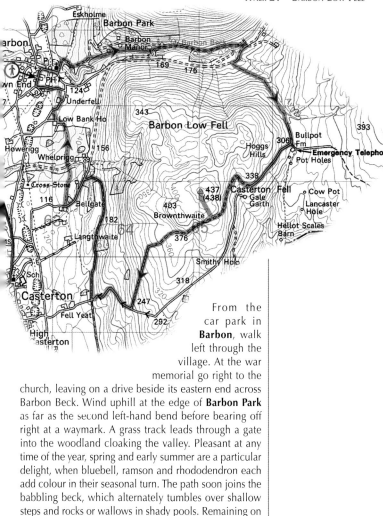

From the car park in **Barbon**, walk left through the village. At the war memorial go right to the church, leaving on a drive beside its eastern end across Barbon Beck. Wind uphill at the edge of **Barbon Park** as far as the second left-hand bend before bearing off right at a waymark. A grass track leads through a gate into the woodland cloaking the valley. Pleasant at any time of the year, spring and early summer are a particular delight, when bluebell, ramson and rhododendron each add colour in their seasonal turn. The path soon joins the babbling beck, which alternately tumbles over shallow steps and rocks or wallows in shady pools. Remaining on this bank, the path eventually breaks out to more open ground, contouring the base of a steep grass slope that rises to Castle Knott. A **footbridge** finally leads across the beck to the Barbondale lane.

Head back down the valley over Blindbeck Bridge, leaving the lane some 200m beyond the bridge along a bridleway signed sharp left to Bullpot. It rises above **Aygill** around the flank of Barbon Low Fell to a low col joining it to the broad ridge from Crag Hill. Just before the crest, the hillside streams gather into the head of Aygill, falling through stony ravines overlooked by the ruin of a lime kiln.

> Looking back there is a fine view along lonely Barbondale, which follows the geological line of the Dent Fault. Past earth movements have uplifted the land to the left by more than 2286m (7500ft), bringing ancient Silurian rocks alongside the more recent carboniferous strata on the eastern side of the valley. Interspersed amongst the layers of limestone and shale within these **carboniferous rocks** are occasional thin seams of coal, which, although of poor quality, were sufficient to fuel the nearby lime kiln to produce fertiliser for the fields.

Through a gate, the way continues as a track, falling between set-back stone walls to the end of a lane opposite **Bullpot Farm**. There is an impressive vista across the valley to Leck Fell, a vast sweep of empty moorland that rises to the long ridge of Gragareth and is broken only by the brighter green of the home pasture below the sprawling farm of Leck Fell House.

Follow the lane to the right along the valley above the deepening fold of Ease Gill, walking for ½ mile (800m) towards **Gale Garth Farm**. Approaching the buildings, look for a gate on the right (the second of two close together), from which a signed grass track strikes onto the fell. After swinging across Gale Beck, it rises around the shoulder of the hill, soon reaching a gate in a lateral wall. To gain the highpoint of the hill without passing through the gate, follow the wall up for ¼ mile (400m) and then move right to the trig pillar at spot height

437m. There is another prospect on the slightly lower top of Brownthwaite, which lies above the path a little further along the track through the gate. However, for those content to remain with the track, there is a fine view along the lower reaches of the River Lune to Morecambe Bay as the way breasts the fell's shoulder. Curving around, Kirkby Lonsdale comes into view, the backdrop to the right being the southern Cumbrian hills.

Whelprigg was built in 1834 for Joseph Gibson's family

Return to continue along the track, which before long swings abruptly through a gate, falling beyond in a straight line to regain the lane. Carry on down the hill for ½ mile (800m), dropping through trees to find a crossing track, **Fellfoot Road**. Follow the track to the right, signed to Bents Lane, as it runs pleasantly along the foot of the hill. Observant eyes will notice a number of small, stiled enclosures beside the path, each containing a boulder. They form part of a landscape sculpture project entitled 'Sheepfolds' created by Andy Goldsworthy.

Turned out at the end onto another lane, go left. After passing a couple of cottages and just before reaching the farm at Fell Garth, leave through a gate on the right. A path signed to Barbon leads away at the edge of a succession of meadows, crossing a final field to a stile beside an avenue of trees dropping from **Whelprigg**, a Victorian mansion built in 1834. Over another stile opposite

continue across the next field, exiting through a gate at
the far corner onto a grass track. It swings round to **Low
Bank House**, but just before entering the farmyard, turn
off beside a barn to a gate. Bear left across the pasture
to a small gate in the corner and keep going until you
emerge onto yet another lane.

Follow it right past a house, but then abandon it on
the bend, walking across the gravel yard of a cottage to a
gate. Carry on at the edge of a meadow to reach an old
contained path at the far side. Go left, shortly crossing the
former railway to emerge at the edge of **Barbon** village.
The village hall is then along to the right.

WALK 22

Around Casterton

Start Point	Devil's Bridge, Kirkby Lonsdale (SD 616 782)
Distance	5¼ miles (8.4km)
Time	2½hrs
Terrain	Tracks and field paths
Height Gain	160m (525ft)
Maps	Explorer OL2 – Yorkshire Dales (Southern and Western areas)
Refreshments	Kirkby Lonsdale and The Pheasant Inn at Casterton
Toilets	By Devil's Bridge
Parking	Devil's Bridge

The small village of Casterton lies above Kirkby Lonsdale beside the former
Ingleton Railway, and offers a short walk from Kirkby Lonsdale onto the
low fringes of Brownthwaite. There are glimpses of the River Lune on the
return, which goes past Casterton Hall. It was the home of Revd Carus-
Wilson, who founded the Clergy Daughters School, to which Patrick
Brontë sent his daughters.

Follow the lane opposite the **Devil's Bridge** east, keeping ahead at the bend up a narrow lane. At the top, turn left along a narrow hedged track beside the entrance to a caravan site. After skirting the site, it later swings to a junction. Go right, ultimately coming out at **High Casterton**.

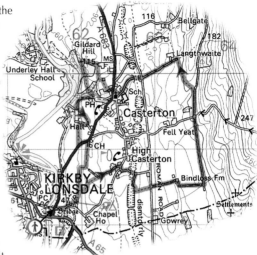

Emerging onto the main lane, walk right and at a fork bear left towards Settle and Cowan Bridge. Just beneath a bridge, built for the now closed Ingleton Railway, turn off right on a track signed to Wandales Lane. Through a gate at the end, strike left past an indented corner and follow the onward hedge out to another lane. This lane follows the course of a Roman road, the Western Way, which connected the forts at Lancaster and Ribchester with Carlisle.

Take the bridleway opposite, signed to Fell Road, which crests a rise to a collection of cottages at **Bindloss Farm**. Bypass them to the right and go through a gate. Turn right along a narrow pasture, at the end of which, swing left on a wide drove towards the higher ground. At the top, follow a broad track, Fellfoot Road, to the left. Along the way look for a sheepfold containing a large boulder on the left, part of a countryside art project created by Andrew Goldsworthy, during which 46 sheepfolds were rebuilt or restored in the years either side of the millennium.

After ½ mile (800m), go over an intersecting lane, the way now signed to Bent's Lane. Stride on for 350m to another of Goldsworthy's sheepfolds, then leave through

Fellfoot Road takes a higher line across the hillside than the Roman road that ran from Lancaster along the Lune Valley and on to Carlisle

a field gate on the left. Bear right across the corner to a stile in the side-wall and maintain the same diagonal line over the crest of a hill to a gate in the far corner. Walk on by the left wall to emerge onto the head of a track and follow it down past **Langthwaite** to a junction of lanes.

The lane opposite winds beneath the dismantled railway to fall past **Casterton School** into the village. Just before the church, turn off right on a short track that drops to the main road.

WILLIAM CARUS-WILSON

The school at Casterton was one of two founded by the Revd William Carus-Wilson, who lived at Casterton Hall. Casterton was for the daughters of servants and teachers, while that at nearby Cowan Bridge was for those of clergymen. In 1824, Patrick Brontë enrolled his four eldest daughters at Cowan Bridge school, but the following year Maria and Elizabeth died during a typhus outbreak, and Charlotte and Emily returned home to Howarth. Charlotte later drew on her unhappy experiences when writing *Jane Eyre*, using the school as a model for Lowood School and basing the tyrannical Mr Brocklehurst upon Carus-Wilson.

Carus-Wilson was incensed when he saw the book and contemplated legal action, but in the event let the matter drop. By then Cowan Bridge had already closed, the two schools being amalgamated at Casterton in 1833. Having moved on from its disreputable history the school now enjoys a fine reputation.

Carus-Wilson also built the church, for the benefit of both the village and the girls attending the two schools. Following its restoration in 1891, Holy Trinity was decorated with paintings commissioned from James Clark and Henry Holiday, who designed the windows too. Holiday, a friend of the Pre-Raphaelites and Ruskin, had made a name for himself producing illustrations for Lewis Carroll.

Take the drive opposite, swinging right after 20m beside Beckside Cottage to pass more school buildings. Keep ahead over a drive and through a gate beside the playing fields. Reaching a ruined barn, curve down left to a gate. Continue up beside a wall on the right behind The Grange. Through a couple of gates, turn left along the edge of a wood down to a kissing-gate. A path leads through the trees and across a pasture into a second wood. Meeting a track at the far side, head right above a stream. At the bottom, a sign points through a gate on the left along the field edge towards Kirkby Lonsdale. Leave left of the corner along a narrow path to meet a drive.

One of Andy Goldsworthy's sheepfolds, part of a seven-year landscape art project completed in 2003

Go right, but just before reaching **Casterton Hall**, exit through a gate on the left. Follow the field edge away, eventually turning out to the main road.

Go left 150m to the entrance of Casterton Golf Course and turn sharp right on a narrow track. Reaching a junction, go right and retrace your outward route back to **Kirkby Lonsdale**.

WALK 23
Kirkby Lonsdale

Start Point	Devil's Bridge, Kirkby Lonsdale (SD 616 782)
Distance	6½ miles (10.5km)
Time	3hrs
Terrain	Lanes, tracks and field paths
Height Gain	160m (525ft)
Maps	Explorer OL2 – Yorkshire Dales (Southern and Western areas)
Refreshments	Kirkby Lonsdale
Toilets	By Devil's Bridge
Parking	Devil's Bridge or, if no space, in Kirkby Lonsdale

The predominance of quiet country lanes, rather than footpaths, in no way detracts from this charming walk around Kirkby Lonsdale, which provides an opportunity to wander through its maze of quaint back streets. After heading into the countryside north of the town, with views across to Barbon Low Fell, the route skirts the Underley estate before returning above the River Lune past a famed Victorian viewpoint.

Cross the Devil's Bridge in **Kirkby Lonsdale** heading towards the town, and bear off right after 100m along a tarmac footpath. Beyond its end, follow the street ahead, eventually reaching a small square dominated by a stone cross, the Swine Market. A narrow ginnel at its far-left corner leads to the churchyard.

KIRKBY LONSDALE

Kirkby Lonsdale was one of the few settlements in the north-west to merit mention in William's great Domesday survey, and even then it had a church. The present building came later, begun around 1090 and decorated with some fine Norman carving, which includes a green man who looks down on the nave from the capital of one of the pillars. The medieval town prospered beside a safe fording point of the river, which became a focus for several packhorse routes. Granted charters in 1227, the town's markets and fair attracted trade, and at one time there were some 30 inns and alehouses catering for the people drawn in each week. Facets of the town's ancient past are revealed in the names of old streets and passageways – Swine Market, Salt Pie Lane, Horse Market and Jingling Lane – although the covered market cross in the Georgian market square is a recent addition from the beginning of the last century.

Leave the churchyard by the tall, wrought iron gates opposite the porch, following Church Street out to Market Street. Go right and then bear left into Mitchelgate. Keep left where that forks along Biggins Road, and pass the school to meet the **A65** road.

Cross to the lane opposite, signed to Burton and Hutton Roof, but then abandon it after ¼ mile (400m) for a path on the right to High Biggins. Head away at the field edge and continue through a wood to come out onto the corner of a lane. Walk forward through the hamlet of **High Biggins** for ½ mile (800m) to a junction and fork right. Immediately mount a stile in the left hedge and cut across the field to emerge at the bottom back on the main road.

Go left and take the next lane on the right to Old Town. Keep ahead at an eventual crossroads, walking a little further to meet the **B6254**. Turn right, but then leave after 200m along a bridleway on the left to Scar Brow. Beyond a pleasant wood, the track passes **Deansbiggin Farm** and finally ends at another lane. Go right, shortly rejoining the classified road at **Kearstwick**.

Now a school, **Underley Hall** was constructed in 1825 for Alexander Nowell and subsequently

One of the magnificent Norman pillars in the church in Kirkby Lonsdale is decorated with a carving of a green man

owned by Thomas Taylour. He was descended from another Thomas Taylour, who had gone to Ireland under Cromwell in the 1650s and held among his titles Earl of Bective. He succeeded his father as MP for Westmorland and served as High Sheriff for the county. The family made many improvements and additions to the hall, including the striking tower, which rises to over 30m, and a bridge across the river connecting the house to the station at Barbon.

Walk left through the hamlet, leaving on the bend along a track signed to Devil's Bridge. Just before a cattle-grid by the Underley estate office, pass through a kissing-gate on the right, from which a path skirts farm buildings to a track. Go right and continue through a small gate down the length of a field. At the far end, swing right over a bridge and, passing through a gate, climb along a wooded bank above the stream. The stream's confluence with the Lune is shrouded in trees, but a little further on the trees give way to reveal a stunning view back along the river.

Ruskin's View – or is it Turner's?

JMW Turner sketched the scene from the church-yard in 1817 and produced a full-sized watercolour that was popularised in an engraving. Ruskin was later so inspired that he came to witness it for him-self and was not disappointed. 'I do not know, in all my own country, still less in France or Italy, a place more naturally divine', and such was his influence that the spot has gone into history as **'Ruskin's View'** and not Turner's.

Just beyond, by the low, crenellated tower of a Georgian folly overlooking the graveyard, turn down a steep stepped path known as the **Radical Steps**. Their name is a reference to the radical Dr Francis Pearson, who lived in the Abbot's Hall beside the Swine Market and later built the cottage by the top of the flight. Wearied by

The Devil's Bridge dates from around 1370

tourists tramping across his property and pilgrims drawn by Ruskin's musing, Turner's picture and Wordsworth's earlier guide, Pearson had the steps constructed to divert the footpath down to the river. The path follows the riverbank past Mill Ayre, a former mill and once the town's gas works, back to **Devil's Bridge**.

WALK 24

By the Lune from Kirkby Lonsdale

Start Point	Devil's Bridge, Kirkby Lonsdale (SD 616 782)
Distance	5¼ miles (8.4km)
Time	2½hrs
Terrain	Tracks and field paths
Height Gain	130m (427ft)
Maps	Explorer OL2 – Yorkshire Dales (Southern and Western areas)
Refreshments	Kirkby Lonsdale and Whittington
Toilets	By Devil's Bridge
Parking	Devil's Bridge or, if no space, in Kirkby Lonsdale

Below Kirkby Lonsdale the character of the Lune changes as the high hills take a step back. The flow broadens and, unless the river is in flood, banks of shingle are exposed, where oystercatchers and other birds stalk. The walk begins over pastoral hills to the nearby village of Whittington and returns along the riverbank, where you might spot a leaping salmon or the iridescent flash of a kingfisher.

DEVIL'S BRIDGE

An attractive market town at the heart of the valley from which it takes its name, Kirkby Lonsdale has one of the best-preserved medieval bridges in the country, the Devil's Bridge, whose graceful arches dramatically straddle the Lune above a rocky cleft. Legend tells that it was built by the Devil at the behest of an old woman, who needed to get to the other bank in search of her strayed cow. As payment, the Devil demanded the soul of the first to cross, and in desperation she agreed. Yet the consequence of her bargain weighed heavily and she began to ponder a way out. Returning next morning with her dog, she found the bridge completed, with the Devil perched on the parapet awaiting his due. Out of her pocket, she took a bun and suddenly flung it over. The dog bounded across after it and, with a wry smile, she slowly followed as the Devil skulked off, no doubt fuming.

You might get your own bun from the snack bar as you leave the car park on the eastern bank, but these days you can eat it yourself and cross with impunity. Immediately over the bridge, go through a squeeze-gap on the left and, following a sign to Biggins, strike a sharp right diagonal to a kissing-gate, concealed behind a couple of evergreens at the far side. Cross the **A65** to another gate and continue over a narrow field to emerge between houses onto a lane. Opposite, the ongoing path, now signed to Wood End, climbs a steep grassy hill. As it draws beside a wall bounding a wood on the left, increasing height opens an expanding rearward view over Casterton to Barbon Low Fell, while to the north Kirkby nestles before a backdrop of Middleton Fell.

Through a gate on the left at the top of the hill, cross the wooded strip and swing right to Wood End

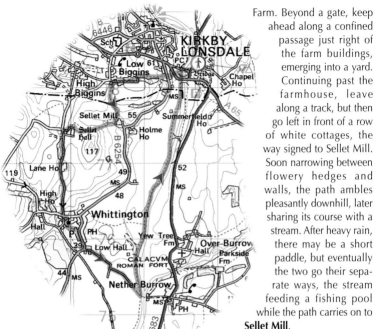

Farm. Beyond a gate, keep ahead along a confined passage just right of the farm buildings, emerging into a yard. Continuing past the farmhouse, leave along a track, but then go left in front of a row of white cottages, the way signed to Sellet Mill. Soon narrowing between flowery hedges and walls, the path ambles pleasantly downhill, later sharing its course with a stream. After heavy rain, there may be a short paddle, but eventually the two go their separate ways, the stream feeding a fishing pool while the path carries on to **Sellet Mill**.

Ingleborough is unmistakable across the valley from Sellet Bank

Entering the yard, go over a stile on the right and walk up the field edge past a house. Just beyond, slip through a gate on the left and cross a narrow pasture to a second gate. Over a stream, curve right around the northern flank of Sellet Bank. Towards the top, as **Sellet Hall** appears, look for a stile in the bordering hedge. Head away, loosely following the left boundary over a rise to leave at a stile beside a junction of lanes.

Stroll left along Hosticle Lane towards **Whittington**, a quiet thoroughfare that winds past Hagg Wood before falling more steeply to the village. At the bottom, go left and then turn into St Michael's Church, which lies within the confines of a Norman bailey. Passing around the building, descend steps below the porch to a stile. Walk beside the extension cemetery and continue at the edge of fields to emerge onto the road at the other side of the village.

> From Whittington came a man whose inventions helped pave the way for our modern world. Born in 1783 and initially apprenticed as a cobbler like his father, **William Sturgeon** joined the army, where he educated himself in mathematics and science and later became a lecturer, instrument maker and inventor. William's passion was electricity, and among his inventions were a viable electromagnet and an electric motor, fundamental components of much of today's electronic equipment. He is honoured by a plaque in Kirkby Lonsdale's church.

Go right, passing the Dragon's Head, but where the road then bends to leave the village turn off to follow a hedged track, Burrow Mill Lane. The way angles lazily between the fields, ultimately leading over a cattle-grid into a field. Keep ahead to a gate at the far side, coming out onto the riverbank opposite the outfall of Leck Beck, whose subterranean source lies beneath the slopes of Crag Hill on the fringe of the Yorkshire Dales.

> Overlooking the confluence here was the Roman fort of **Calacum**, which is said to mean 'basket of

Whittington's church stands on the site of a Norman motte

flowers' and perhaps refers to it being surrounded by flower meadows. The fort stood beside the Western Way, a Roman road that ran between Lancashire and Carlisle and was mentioned by the geographer Ptolemy in the second century.

Turning upstream, follow a riverside path through a succession of grazing meadows, eventually passing a bridge that is part of the 80-mile (129km) Haweswater aqueduct, which carries about 10 million gallons of water a day to Manchester. The water flows entirely by gravity, and further south tunnels deep below the Bowland hills. Half a mile (800m) further on, the path ends beside the **A65** road bridge. Cross the road and walk back to the **Devil's Bridge**.

WALK 25
Leck Beck

Start Point	Cowan Bridge (SD 635 764)
Distance	8½ miles (13.7km)
Time	3½hrs
Terrain	Bouldery paths
Height Gain	360m (1181ft)
Maps	Explorer OL2 – Yorkshire Dales (Southern and Western areas)
Refreshments	None
Toilets	None
Parking	Car park by village hall (donation)

Leck Fell and the gorge of Ease Gill, which joins Leck Beck near its source, are more familiar to cavers than walkers, for this is limestone country and the whole area is peppered with pots, holes, caverns and sinks. But although the real treasures lie deep underground, accessible only by the specialists, there is plenty to see on top. This there-and-back walk through the valley is set against a backdrop of moorland hills and leads to some of the area's most fascinating geological features. Much of the walk is on regular paths, but care is necessary when exploring Ease Gill gorge and the bouldery riverbed of the dry valley.

Leaving the car park by **Cowan Bridge** village hall, return to the main road and walk a short distance right before leaving the road over a stile, just before the bridge from which the village takes its name. Follow Leck Beck upstream, passing beneath the former Ingleton Railway. In the third field beyond the bridge, swing right and cross another field to emerge in **Leck**. Go left, keeping ahead past junctions, with the lane eventually degrading to a track. Entering a meadow beyond Low Beck House, amble on, in time crossing a stream and branching left to Springs Wood.

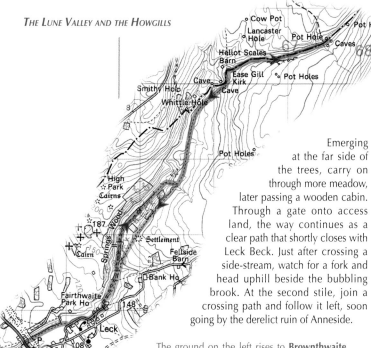

Emerging at the far side of the trees, carry on through more meadow, later passing a wooden cabin. Through a gate onto access land, the way continues as a clear path that shortly closes with Leck Beck. Just after crossing a side-stream, watch for a fork and head uphill beside the bubbling brook. At the second stile, join a crossing path and follow it left, soon going by the derelict ruin of Anneside.

The ground on the left rises to **Brownthwaite**, where the slopes bear traces of prehistoric settlement from Neolithic to Roman times. Ahead the ground rises to distant Crag Hill and Great Coum, while over to the right, Leck Fell climbs to **Gragareth**, now the highest point in Lancashire since The Old Man of Coniston was incorporated into Cumbria during the reorganisation of local government boundaries in 1974. Eagle eyes might catch a glimpse of Gragareth's Three Men, an impressive group of stone pillars that stand on the flank below the summit.

Beyond a broken wall, the path briefly dips to ford a stream and then continues as before, later crossing a ladder-stile and another broken wall. Below, Leck Beck's valley quickly narrows to a deep fold where the water is churned white over low falls, for just upstream it has burst out of the ground – not as a gentle spring, but as a full-fledged flow.

134

The streambed above the waterfall at Cow Holes has been sculpted by the water

Some 300m after the wall, branch off the main path for a view into the dramatic gorge of **Ease Gill Kirk**. It is possible to clamber down the steep grass bank to explore the dry riverbed, but go carefully, particularly when it is wet. The stream disappears underground over a mile (1.6km) higher up the valley, revealing the smooth, sculpted ledges of waterfalls and spouts. Occasionally, after very heavy rain, the pots upstream are unable to take all the water, and the flow can surge through the gully with phenomenal force.

PLUMBING THE DEPTHS

Although the many pots and caves dotted around the hillside have been known since antiquity, the full extent and interconnectivity of the underground passageways and streams have been realised only during the last 60 years or so. Interest was sparked in the latter part of the 19th century by guidebook descriptions of some of the holes, prompting members of the recently formed Yorkshire Ramblers Club to begin exploration.

The first recorded descent was into Bull Pot of the Witches in 1899, which was discovered to be 64m (210ft) deep. Other tentative expeditions followed, and by the 1930s systematic investigation was underway. During the years of the Second World War, little further work was possible, but the discovery of Lancaster Hole in 1946 began a fresh wave of exploration. The development of new techniques, particularly cave diving, gave access to previously impossible passages, and now more than 47 miles (76km) of subterranean tunnels have been mapped to reveal the longest and most complex natural underground system in Britain.

Passage upstream is impeded by the abrupt cliff of a dry waterfall, so return to the top path and carry on for another 200m to bypass it before clambering down once more into the valley. The descent here is much easier, allowing more exploration, but upriver progress is again obstructed by a fall. Briefly rejoin the upper path then drop to the riverbed for a final time. There, continue upstream over the dry boulders (crossing occasional fences) for almost a mile (1.6km), the valley floor sporadically widening to accommodate narrow borders of flower meadow.

Ultimately, at Cow Holes, the way is again blocked by a fall, hidden within a narrow cleft, but this time water tumbles over the lip into a deep pool and is immediately swallowed underground. All is not quite over, for there is just one more fascinating sight. Just before the fall, clamber out of the valley to the right to have a look at the channel that the stream has carved from the solid rock above.

The way back simply reverses the outward route, although beyond Anneside Farm an alternative path continues ahead along the valley side. It is not as picturesque as the outward path, but does have the advantage of passing below the late prehistoric settlement of Castle Hill. To

Looking back down the dry bed of Ease Gill from above Cow Holes

follow the alternative route, keep ahead past the stile along a moorland path, eventually curving to a gate by a plantation and pheasant pens. Instead of passing through, carry on a little further to a ladder-stile. Sticking with the wall, the way soon passes onto lusher pasture and steadily loses height below the settlement site. Keep going until you reach a ladder-stile on the right, which returns you to the outward path just before it meets the lane at Low Beck House.

WALK 26
Arkholme and the River Lune

Start Point	Arkholme (SD 584 721)
Distance	6¾ miles (10.9km)
Time	3hrs
Terrain	Field paths and lanes
Height Gain	180m (591ft)
Maps	Explorer OL2 – Yorkshire Dales (Southern and Western areas) and Explorer OL7 – English Lakes (South Eastern area)
Refreshments	The Bay Horse at Arkholme
Toilets	None
Parking	Car park by village hall

Beginning from Arkholme, overlooking an ancient ford across the River Lune, this pleasant ramble circles north to the nearby hamlet of Newton. The way returns through the open grazing meadows beside the river.

In **Arkholme** walk to the crossroads by The Bay Horse and go right towards Docker. After 250m, just past the last of the cottages, take a tarmac track on the left, but then immediately leave through a gate on the right. Climb by the hedge, slipping through a gap in the corner to find a narrow squeeze-stile at the top of the hill. Strike half-right down the hill to a gate beside a junction of lanes.

ARKHOLME

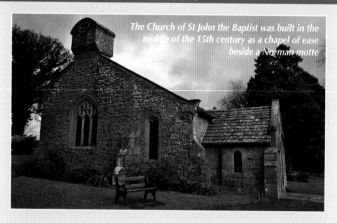

The Church of St John the Baptist was built in the middle of the 15th century as a chapel of ease beside a Norman motte

Arkholme is an attractive village of rough-stone cottages, many dating from the growth in farming prosperity during the 17th century. But its origins are far older, having evolved beside a ford across the River Lune, and it was originally known as Erwhum. The ford brought trade, and the lord of the manor was granted a charter for a weekly market and annual fair under Edward I in 1279. The crossing was guarded by a motte, which may even predate the Normans and is now known as Chapel Hill, for beside it is the village church.

Dedicated to St John the Baptist, the church dates from the middle of the 15th century and was built as a chapel of ease to Melling. Until 1866, when Arkholme became a parish in its own right, the dead had to be carried across the ford for burial in the churchyard there. Like most churches, it has been altered over the years, but there has never been enough money to furnish it with a tower. Its bell is said to be one of the oldest in England and hangs within the bulbous belfry perched upon the apex of the west wall.

Take the minor lane on the left, marked as a cul-de-sac. After passing a track off to **Craven View**, enter the fields through the next gate on the left. Cross to a stile part-way along the distant end-wall and continue to the far right corner of the next field. Walk on to a stile on the right and keep going on the other side of the fence, passing through a gate to the top of the hill. Reaching a signpost by sheds at **High Farm**, go over a stile to the right. Cross a track and stride down to another finger-post in the bottom-left corner. Of the two stiles there, mount the one on the left and, looking out for the stiles breaking the intervening boundaries, head away across successive fields, eventually reaching a lane.

Follow it right for ½ mile (800m) before abandoning it on a bend, just past **Docker Park Farm**. Walk away at the edge

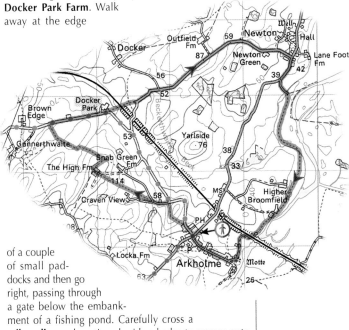

of a couple of small paddocks and then go right, passing through a gate below the embankment of a fishing pond. Carefully cross a **railway line** and continue beside a hedge to emerge onto a lane. Follow it to the left, until it eventually reaches the main road at **Newton**, 1½ miles (2.4km) away.

Around **Newton** curlew and lapwing are often to be heard and seen in the fields, their cries among the more easily identified of the grassland birds. In the distance, east of north, is Barbon Low Fell, while further to the right rises Ingleborough, easily recognised by its distinctive steep-sided, flat-topped summit. As the road bends to the hamlet, there is a glimpse across the fields to the River Lune.

Turn right towards Arkholme and Carnforth, but be mindful of traffic, for this lane is busier than the last. Shortly, where the lane bends right, turn off along a track on the left. It leads to riverside grazing, where the screech of the oystercatcher prevails. Through a gate at the bottom, bear right to strike a course parallel to the riverbank. After some ½ mile (800m), move away to a footbridge. Head half-left to a stile and continue in the same direction beyond beside a string of wooded pools marking a former course of the river.

Over a second bridge, bear right on a rising track to Lower Broomfield Farm. Keep ahead past the barns and farmhouse, then slip over a stile on the left immediately past a Nissen-style shed. Entering a field, climb away at the edge, but part-way along hop over a stile and continue above wooded banking that falls to the river. Approaching a **bridge**, the way drops beneath the end arch. It is part of a ¾-mile (1.2km) viaduct that was built in 1867 by the Furness and Midland Joint Railway to link

Old stone barns at Lower Broomfield

the iron-rich, but far-flung detached corner of Lancashire, Furness, with Yorkshire.

A track beside the embankment leads away from the river. Swing left in front of a gate to skirt a delightful wetland wood full of ransom, wood anemone, flag iris and celandine. Willows growing here once sustained a basket-weaving industry, one of the traditional occupations for the villagers of Arkholme. Beyond the wood the track winds around a cottage to the church at **Arkholme**. Keep going to join the main lane, which leads back to the crossroads by The Bay Horse.

WALK 27
Melling

Start Point	Loyn Bridge (SD 580 697)
Distance	5½ miles (8.8km)
Time	2½hrs
Terrain	Field paths
Height Gain	145m (476ft)
Maps	Explorer OL2 – Yorkshire Dales (Southern and Western areas)
Refreshments	None
Toilets	None
Parking	Roadside parking west of Loyn Bridge

Between Kirkby Lonsdale and Crook o'Lune the ancient river cut a broad swathe between the hills – it is far too wide for today's Lune, which wanders this way and that between the extensive meadows that now fill the valley's base. Over time the river's meandering path has changed, and old banks and stranded pools give clues to former lines of flow. Even now the river can suddenly flood extensive areas, leaving stranded tree trunks and debris washed against fences as testament to its power. After climbing onto the hill above Melling for views across the main valley and into the neighbouring dale of Wenning, the walk returns along that expansive flood plain beside a former course of the Lune.

Castle Stede is one of the best preserved motte and bailey castles in Lancashire

A FORTIFIED LANDSCAPE

Although gently pastoral today, this section of valley was once one of the most heavily fortified places in the country, with eight early Norman castles in the 14 miles (22.5km) between Lancaster and Kirkby Lonsdale. All but the castle at Lancaster were subsequently abandoned and exist now only as mottes – earth mounds upon which a defensible stronghold or keep was perched. Many became the focus of a medieval village, with the church being built on or close to the mound, perhaps having evolved from the original castle chapel.

Castle Stede, near Loyn Bridge, was deserted after the construction of Hornby Castle at the beginning of the 13th century, so the village grew up at Hornby instead. The earthworks of Castle Stede, however, remain vivid, and it is one of the best examples of a motte and bailey in Lancashire. It was built to oversee a fording point of the river, its strategic situation being re-emphasised nine centuries later with the construction of a pill box there during the Second World War.

Loyn Bridge is classified as an ancient monument and dates from around 1684, being built to replace an earlier structure that had become dangerous. The wide arches and massive cutwaters have helped it stand the test of time and the torrential floods that occasionally sweep down the valley.

Cross **Loyn Bridge**, leaving just around the bend through a squeeze-stile on the left. Head up past the pill box and mound of Castle Stede, dropping beyond beside the wall to pass through gates onto a concrete farm track. Walk ahead, but immediately slip through a gate on the left and carry on beside the left hedge. As that then falls away, keep an elevated line to leave at the far corner onto the main road (**A683**).

Follow the verge right for 200m, passing a milestone before crossing to a gate. Many milestones such as this were erected during the 18th century with the development of turnpike roads. Strike a left diagonal upfield past a twisted oak and carry on above a **wood**. Passing through a gate, parallel the right-hand wall, swinging through the second of two gates just before the crest of the hill. Although the trig column beckons ahead, the way curves back left across the large field, making for a ladder-stile at its distant corner. The height enables an extensive view up the valley – Ingleborough is unmistakable, while further left are Whernside, Great Coum and Middleton Fell.

Follow a fence down to a gate, slipping through to continue on the other side through a belt of trees. Over a stile at the far side, walk the length of a field to a gate and amble on by the right-hand fence down to **Park House Farm**. Exiting the field, go sharp left past the barns, continuing beyond on a track above a wood. Keep

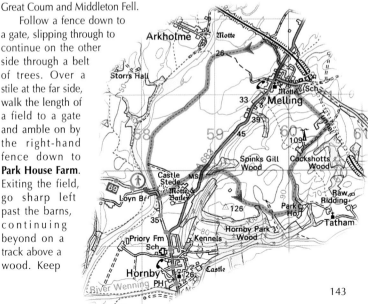

There are numerous 18th-century milestones throughout the area dating from the time of the turnpikes

going at the field edge, eventually crossing a stile. Carry on to **Lodge Farm** at the top of the hill.

Walk forward through a gate at the side of the farmhouse, passing through the yard to leave on a metalled track. Some 200m after a cattle-grid, mid-way between two large mounds set back either side of the track, abandon the track and strike out left to seek a stile by the corner of a clump of trees. Beneath your feet is the **Melling Tunnel**, which was built about 1865 to carry the Furness and Midland Joint Railway beneath the hill. The two mounds are heaps of spoil that were excavated during its construction.

Bearing slightly left, head downfield to find a stile part-way along the bottom fence. Keep going across the next field and, tending to the left boundary, slip over a stile halfway along to continue on its opposite flank. Exiting at the bottom corner, walk out to a lane and go left to a junction with the main road in **Melling**.

> **St Wilfrid's Church** in Melling lies just to the left along the main road and is a 14th-century replacement for the original church, which was possibly Anglo-Saxon but was destroyed by Scottish raiders in 1322. Built beside a Norman motte, the church was once known as the 'Cathedral of the Valley' and served not only this village but Arkholme too, for until the middle of the 19th century their dead were brought across the river for burial in the churchyard here.

The onward way at the junction with the main road is to the right. At the edge of the village branch left onto a gravel track, but, approaching a bridge, turn left along a grass track that ends at a field gate. Walk on by the left fence at the edge of a sparse, wet woodland, which borders a former channel of the Lune. Over a couple of stiles, continue past a reedy pool to follow the old riverbank.

Eventually reach a vague crossing track by a large, waymarked ash tree and swing left. Keep going above the old line of the river, later passing through successive gates

and crossing a stream. A developing track heads towards a flood bank, but ignore the gate and instead carry on beside the fence along the elevated embankment, which runs for ¾ mile (1.2km) back to **Loyn Bridge**.

Reed-filled pools mark a former course of the River Lune near Melling

WALK 28

Roeburndale

Start Point	By Barkin Bridge (SD 600 638)
Distance	8 miles (12.9km)
Time	4hrs
Terrain	Woodland and indistinct moorland paths
Height Gain	442m (1450ft)
Maps	Explorer OL41 – Forest of Bowland and Ribblesdale
Refreshments	None
Toilets	None
Parking	Roadside parking north of Barkin Bridge

Although Bowland's upland moors have not been forested since prehistoric times, the deep valleys remain wooded, and one of the largest areas of ancient semi-natural woodland surviving in Lancashire is in Roeburndale. Throughout the Middle Ages the Forest of Bowland was a royal hunting ground, and much of the area continues in the ownership of the crown as part of the Duchy of Lancaster. With names like Buckbank Wood, Hunts Gill, Bowskill Wood and Roeburn itself, this corner must have been well stocked with deer and a favourite with the huntsmen. The deer are still here, and if you go quietly through the woods you may see them.

The River Roeburn below Outhwaite Wood

Leave the lane over a stile just north of **Barkin Bridge**. Strike diagonally across the pasture, climb to a fence-stile at the top of the bank and go right above the deep river gorge. After passing through a gate and reaching the corner of the fence, drop right to a field gate, from which a grass track slants back through trees into the valley. At the bottom, swing downstream into a broad-ening meadow, crossing a footbridge over the **River Roeburn** beyond its far end.

On 8 August 1967 the narrow valley was inundated by a **flash flood** that followed a short but torrential downpour. The moors were unable to absorb the water, and the sudden run-off was channelled into the deep, constricted valleys radiating from the hills. Thundering through the valley, the waters stripped away trees and bridges and demolished a number of cottages at Wray, although miraculously no one was killed.

Ignoring the gate, continue downstream beside the river, watching for a waymark that soon directs the path up the bank to a stile. Climb by the left fence, and at the top of the bank dip left across a side-stream. Occasional waymarks guide you around the fields above the convoluted boundary of the wood, eventually crossing another stile and stream. Clamber out of the gully and over a wall-stile to follow a path into **Outhwaite Wood**, which in spring is thickly carpeted with bluebells. Watch for a waypost later steering you left, the path now gently losing height and passing a small clearing, from which there is a stunning view back up the valley. Not far beyond, fork left, the way winding down more steeply to meet a track along the bottom of the valley.

After 100m, at a kink in the track, branch right on a narrow path along the foot of a wooded bank where heady ransoms

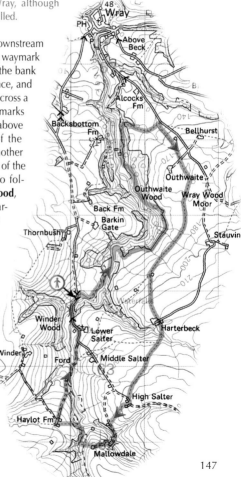

147

flower in spring. Ignore a later crossing track from a meadow below and continue through a tall gate. A little further on, drop through a kissing-gate to a track through the meadow. At the far end, join a path from a bridge across the river, which leads to three gates in the corner. Take the middle one (not the bridleway) and follow a footpath through the trees. Emerging at the top, carry on across a couple of fields, and then at the edge of a third a view opens left to Great Coum and Middleton Fell.

Entering a small pasture, the final one before reaching a lane, look for a stone stile to the right. Heading upfield, Ingleborough now appears in the distance over to the left, while in front are the Bowland fells. Pass into the next field beside a barn and leave at the top over a

Harterbeck Farm

stile by a stream onto a track near **Outhwaite Farm**. Cross and stride on from field to field beside the left boundary, eventually, after some ¾ mile (1.2km), passing a lone tree. With the line of the wall now all but gone, bear slightly left to a wall-stile. Keep going to a ladder-stile by a barn, where the path splits. Branch left, walking up the field edge to find a kissing-gate in a shallow corner. Head out over a final field, passing left of **Harterbeck Farm** to come out onto a track.

Go right and immediately left beside a barn. Walk down to a stream and take the right fork. Where the track then bends, bear off right, slanting down to a footbridge spanning Goodber Beck. The path climbs away onto a high bank, where to the right is a view of a fine waterfall as the stream tumbles into the narrow gorge of Peddar Gill. The onward path, however, is over to the left and follows a fence to a gate and stile. Bear right to a wall-stile near the top corner and walk on, maintaining your direction as the left wall then moves away towards a fence-stile. Strike across the next field and, over a couple of stiles, continue to **High Salter Farm**.

Follow the track left past the farm, leaving after 100m for a field gate over to the right. Walk downhill by the boundary to a lane at the bottom, which, to the left, descends to the River Roeburn at Mallowdale Bridge. Climb away to **Mallowdale Farm**, leaving over a stile on the right just before the buildings. Contour below the farm to the end of a wall and drop steeply to a footbridge at the confluence of Mallow Gill and Lambclose Syke.

Head up to the right across the steep bank of Melling Wood. Emerging into a field at the top, follow the perimeter right. Cross a stile at the corner and head left up to **Haylot Farm**. Turn right to leave the yard and go right again. Where the track then immediately splits, keep ahead through a gate along the lane signed to Roeburndale. After crossing the River Roeburn again at Irish Bridge, climb over a rise to join the lane from High Salter. Continue past the Methodist chapel at **Lower Salter** and drop back to **Barkin Bridge**.

WALK 29

Whit Moor

Start Point	Claughton Quarry (SD 570 643)
Distance	6¼ miles (10.1km)
Time	3hrs
Terrain	Open moor and upland tracks
Height Gain	300m (984ft)
Maps	Explorer OL41 – Forest of Bowland and Ribblesdale
Refreshments	None
Toilets	None
Parking	Car park at Claughton Quarry
Note	The route is not recommended for inexperienced walkers in poor visibility, when map and compass are essential.

Throughout its length the River Lune has been intimately connected with the hills from which it draws sustenance, and here in its latter stages it skirts the very foot of the Bowland fells. This walk begins from a superb viewpoint on the edge of the moors above Claughton and then climbs over the lonely hill to peek into Roeburndale.

The **wind turbines** on Caton Moor are a dominating landmark, a feature that is becoming increasingly common on Britain's hills as the move towards 'green power' gathers momentum. While the windmills of yesteryear have acquired a certain nostalgic charm, today's equivalent has still to gain that universal appeal, yet the slender towers and slightly hypnotic rotation of the blades have an aesthetic elegance that adds yet another dimension to the country's ever-changing landscape. Commissioned in 1994, Caton Moor was one of the first commercial wind farm sites in the country. Since then, the ten original towers have been replaced with eight more powerful turbines, which have a collective maximum output of 16 megawatts, enough to power 10,000 homes.

The Caton Moor wind farm was one of the earliest such developments in the country

Go through the gate just beyond the quarry car park, from which a bridleway is signed, but then immediately turn right through a second gate and follow a rising track beside the **wind-farm** site.

> The surrounding mounds and hollows remain from **Claughton Quarry**, which provided sandstone slabs for paving and roofing flags. A little further to the north is a more extensive quarry that supplied shale to Manor Brickworks in the valley below. The factory opened towards the end of the 19th century, and clay was transported down the hill by two gravity-powered aerial ropeways. One was dismantled after the western works closed in 1990, but the

other remains operational. The line runs over 1¼ miles (2km) and is capable of carrying 250 tons of shale a day. At the time of writing, however, the factory, owned by Hansons, had been mothballed due to a decline in the demand for bricks.

Pass through a gateway at the crest and immediately turn off left along a faint trod by the wall, passing a guyed mast whose instruments gather wind-speed data to assist in planning the wind farm's development. Shortly after, watch for a fork and take the right branch, which leads to a trig column. Bear left on a trod, marked by intermittent wooden posts, which takes you back to the wall. Pass through a fence gate and turn half-right, the way again occasionally marked by a post. With Warmbeck Gill falling to the right, the trod eventually leads to another gate. Without going through, turn left beside the fence, which later curves to the right and falls to a wall. Despite the apparent emptiness of the moor, there are often many birds about. In spring, the calls of lapwing, curlew and skylark can fill the air, and you might catch sight of a golden plover or hawk.

Go through a kissing-gate to the left and follow a track beside the wall. As the wall then curves right, bear off to pick up another sporadic line of posts that

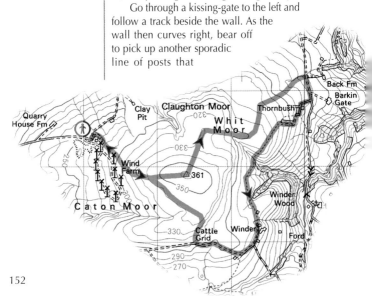

A windbreak of Scots Pine above Thornbush Farm

steers you to a field gate in a lower fence. Through that strike half-left and carry on downhill, ultimately leaving the moor through a kissing-gate at the far bottom corner onto a lane.

Walk right along the lane for nearly ¼ mile (400m) before turning off up to **Thornbush Farm**. Pass through the farmyard and wind away along a rising field track. Go through a gate at the foot of a belt of pine trees and swing up beside them to another gate at the top corner. The onward track curves left, eventually leading to a pair of gates. Take that on the left and carry on beside the fence. Beyond its corner, bear slightly left of a furrow in the ground, soon losing height to find a stile in a stone wall.

Drop into a deep gully to cross **Warm Beck**, where trees have been planted to help stabilise the crumbling shale of the steep slopes. Climb left to a kissing-gate at the top of the bank and, guided by more posts, head across the moss. Walk beyond another kissing-gate and shortly cross a collapsed wall to pick up a rough track that leads to a gate below a belt of conifers. The onward track runs past a barn down to the farm at **Winder**.

Following the lane away, keep ahead at a junction. After another ½ mile (800m), abandon the lane at a cattle-grid for a track on the right that climbs beside a wall onto the moor and opens a superb view across Roeburndale. After swinging left at the top, the track soon crests the hill and descends back past the **wind farm** to the parking area.

WALK 30
Littledale

Start Point	Rigg Lane car park, Quernmore (SD 526 604)
Distance	8¼ miles (13.3km)
Time	4hrs
Terrain	Heath and field paths, lanes
Height Gain	385m (1263ft)
Maps	Explorer OL41 – Forest of Bowland and Ribblesdale
Refreshments	None
Toilets	None
Parking	Car park at start

Tucked beneath the steep northern slopes of Clougha, Littledale is another of Bowland's treasures. This walk skirts the moorland flanks before dropping to cross Artle Beck, the stream flowing at its base. A quiet path wanders up the valley, ultimately cresting a low pass into Roeburndale. But you need only go as far as you wish before returning along the valley to complete the circle back to the car park.

Leave the car park in **Quernmore** through the gate at the back of the car park, keeping left when the track forks to follow a grassy path below the over-grown quarries of Birk Bank. Cross Ottergear Bridge, which carries the aqueduct from Thirlmere across a deep clough, and bear left to continue with the main track. Reaching a gravel

track, turn right towards the moor. The track meanders into a gully and, after passing through a gate, climbs to a sharp bend.

Abandon the track for a narrow but distinct path that contours across the sloping heath above **Cragg Wood**. After passing a clump of oak, the path loses height,

Contouring the hillside above Cragg Wood

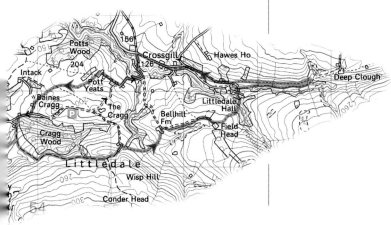

crossing a couple of streams on its way towards the head of the valley. Reaching a ladder-stile, cross and walk to the right above Sweet Beck. At a junction beyond a second stile, go right, bridging the beck to head away by a fence on the right. Mounting a stile by a gate, follow a rough track down left to a bridge beside Wisp Ford and climb away towards **Bellhill Farm**. Walk between the farm and converted outbuildings to meet the end of a metalled track and go right over a cattle-grid. The farm track undulates to the next farm, **Field Head**.

On the approach to the buildings a sign directs right, cutting the field corner behind the farm to a wall-stile. Over that, turn left and walk down to a stile into the wood. The path falls sharply through the trees to a bridge spanning **Foxdale Beck**. Head briefly downstream on the opposite bank before the path turns into a farmyard. Wind through the yard and down towards **Littledale Farm**, turning right just before the buildings to cross Artle Beck. The ongoing route leads up the valley for ¾ mile (1.2km), returning here along a higher parallel path.

If not pressed for time, you can wander even further upstream to the head of Deep Clough, overlooking Roeburndale, but then come back to this point.

The way back to Quernmore continues beside the wall down the valley, soon passing a redundant Victorian chapel, built in 1849 and now used to store farming paraphernalia. Keep going through a wood to emerge on the corner of lane.

The tiny **chapel** was built by the Revd John Dodson, formerly vicar of Cockerham, who, like several others, turned his back on the established church following the Gorham Judgement in 1849. George Gorham, an Anglican priest, successfully appealed to a secular court against an ecclesiastical decision that his beliefs on baptismal regeneration rendered him unsuitable for the appointment as vicar of Brampford Speke in Devon. Dodson, the son of a Liverpool shipowner, held the Littledale estate and

The Revd John Dodson's Free Church

built this Free Church, where he served as minister until his death in 1890.

Walk left, passing **Crossgill**, and shortly reaching a junction at New House. Again go left, dropping to successive bridges across the river and Udale Beck. Follow the lane steeply away. Higher up, after crossing a cattle-grid, turn off right on a track to **Pott Yeats Farm**. Follow the track into the top yard and exit through a gateway beside a barn. Walk away at the field edge, continuing forward into the next field. Go through another gate and keep going by the wall, later curving left into the narrowing tail of the field to find a stile over to the left. A rough trod guides you on, crossing a peaty stream to another stile. Over that, go left, soon emerging onto **Littledale Road**.

Head downhill, leaving after some 300m over a stile on the left. A path falls through bracken to the River Conder, beyond which, join a rising track to a gate. Through that turn right and retrace your outward route over Ottergear Bridge and below the Birk Bank quarries to the car park in **Quernmore**.

WALK 31
Clougha Pike

Start Point	Rigg Lane car park, Quernmore (SD 526 604)
Distance	5½ miles (8.8km)
Time	2¾hrs
Terrain	Rough moorland paths
Height Gain	365m (1197ft)
Maps	Explorer OL41 – Forest of Bowland and Ribblesdale
Refreshments	None
Toilets	None
Parking	Car park at start

Clougha Pike is a beckoning hill just to the east of Lancaster, above the village of Quernmore, and marks the edge of the Bowland fells overlooking the head of the Conder Valley. The lower slopes of the hill are littered with the debris of quarrying, once an important activity in the area. The rough stone was particularly suited for the manufacture of millstones, and the name of the village has its root in 'quern', an ancient type of hand-mill used for grinding corn. Slate quarrying and even coal mining were also carried out in the area, as was the earlier manufacture of pottery by the Romans, the site of a kiln being marked on the OS map about 1 mile (1.6km) to the south of the car park.

Begin along a gravel track through a gate at the back of the car park in **Quernmore**. At a fork keep right and then right again. Approaching a gate drop left to a duckboarded path across the boggy head of a stream. Beyond, the path rises through trees, with a babbling stream, largely unseen, cascading over to the right. The trees dwindle to heath as the path gradually gains height and before long arrives at adjacent stiles. Over the one on the right, carry on by the left wall, later cutting within its corner. The high ground of Clougha then shortly reveals itself.

Passing through a wicket gate, pause for the view behind, a foretaste of that from the top. The ongoing trod

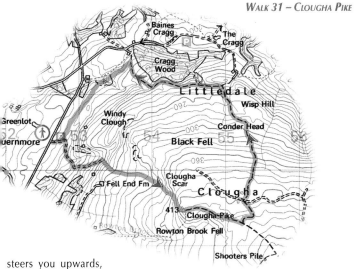

steers you upwards,
clambering over boulders
of hard gritty stone. Reaching a second
gate, go through and then immediately over a stile on the
right to head towards a prominent cairn. Beyond that, the
trig column on **Clougha Pike** comes into view.

There is a superb view from the top of Clougha

Despite its modest height on the edge of the Bowland massif, **Clougha** is a grand viewpoint, and on a good day you can see past the southern Lakeland fells to the Isle of Man, out to the Yorkshire Dales and down to the Clwydian range in Wales.

From the trig column, the onward path swings to the left, making slightly north of east. Cross a fence-stile and continue across the upland heath for almost another ¼ mile (400m) to find a fork in a slight dip. Take the left branch, now heading more generally north towards the distant wind turbines of the Caton Wind Farm. Reaching a gravel track, cross and maintain your direction, the way shortly beginning to lose height in earnest. A wall later comes in from the right, while a stream, the infant River Conder, delves through a deepening gully over to the left. The path falls beside it into the head of **Littledale**.

At the bottom, go left, crossing the stream and picking up an undulating path along the sloping valley side. It shortly rises past a clump of oak trees to a fork. Stay with the right branch, the path choosing an easy course across the hillside above **Cragg Wood**. Eventually reaching a gravel track, go right, dropping through a rocky ravine to a gate. Carry on until the route approaches a second gate, and leave the track just before it to follow a broad grassy path to the left. After crossing Ottergear Bridge, which carries the Thirlmere Aqueduct, continue with the wandering track past shattered quarry debris below Birk Bank. Keep generally ahead on the main path, which ultimately returns you to the Rigg Lane car park at **Quernmore**.

WALK 32

Aughton and the River Lune

Start Point	Crook o'Lune (SD 521 647)
Distance	7¼ miles (11.7km)
Time	3¼hrs
Terrain	Riverside and field paths
Height Gain	195m (640ft)
Maps	Explorer OL41 – Forest of Bowland and Ribblesdale
Refreshments	Seasonal café at start
Toilets	At start
Parking	Car park at start

At the Crook o'Lune, the Lune is pinched within a narrow gorge. Upstream, in contrast, it snakes over bars of gravel in a broad, flat-bottomed valley of grazing meadows, framed between rising hills that focus the eye upon the distant heights of the Yorkshire Dales. Tacking across the steeper slopes above the river's northern bank, this route exploits these views to the full. After dropping through the pretty hamlet of Aughton, the walk returns beside the river, culminating in a delightful stretch through remnants of ancient woodland.

Begin from the rear of the overspill car park at the **Crook o'Lune** along a contained path beside the road. Emerging at the end, go right along Park Lane. The first of many vistas opens across the valley to Caton Moor and the western fringes of the Bowland hills, while the distinctive mountain straight ahead is Ingleborough.

CATON AND LOW MILL

The old village of Caton was clustered around the Norman church between two streams, Bull Beck and Kirk Beck, but extended westward after Low Mill was built at Town End in 1784. About half the labour force was made up of orphaned children brought from Liverpool, and although they worked long hours, the owner, Thomas Hodgson, was a considerate employer for his time and provided for their care with an apprentice house, meals and even a school master.

Used for spinning cotton, the mill was later taken over by Samuel Greg, a highly successful Manchester businessman who owned several other mills including Quarry Bank at Styal, which is now cared for by the National Trust. Rebuilt after a fire in 1838, Low Mill continued in production until 1970 and has since been converted into dwellings. At one time there were five mills operating in the village, producing cotton, silk and flax.

Later climbing between hedges, the lane leads to **Halton Park Farm** and turns from the main valley. After some ¼ mile (400m) abandon it for a track on the right that rises through trees to **Hawkshead Farm**. Approaching the yard, watch for a stile on the left beside a barn.

The path skirts the meadow above the farm to another stile by a derelict oak. Carry on along the opposite flank of the hedge, continuing beyond the corner to a kissing-gate into a wood, where foxglove,

Hawkshead Farm

162

herb robert and ragged robin all
bloom in early summer. At the
far side of the trees, cross a
small meadow to a field
gate and head up to
**Lower Highfield
Farm**.

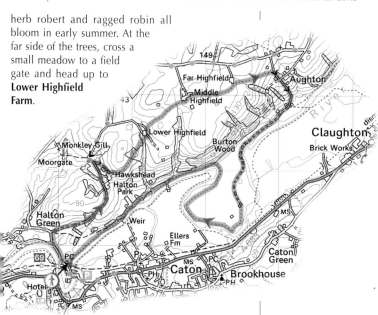

At the top of the yard,
bear right in front of a barn and
walk up through the gate ahead. Follow the field perimeter left until it reaches a signpost, and then cut the corner
to a gate. Bear left to a ladder-stile and carry on by the left
boundary to the next farm, **Middle Highfield**.

Leaving the field over a stile beside a gate, briefly go
left along the drive to find a narrow cobbled passage on
the right. Cross a gravel drive and stile to pass another
cottage and keep ahead through a gate by sheds across
the paddock beyond. Over a stile at the far side, follow
the left boundary beside more fields to **Far Highfield**.

Bypass the buildings to a stile and bear right down
the field, crossing a bridged ditch to reach another stile.
Head out of the corner in a slanting descent, aiming for a
stile to the left of a couple of trees. Carry on across a final
pasture to emerge onto a lane.

The view up the River Lune from opposite Low Mill

Walk downhill to a junction in **Aughton** and continue along the narrow lane opposite, which drops ever more steeply into the valley. Swinging past a cottage at the bottom it degrades to a track and heads across meadows flanking the River Lune. The way courts the river for a while, but later, occasional posts mark a course set back on slightly higher ground that curves to Over Lune Barn. Rejoin the river as it squirms a convoluted course, eventually returning to the foot of the scar defining the northern flank of the valley. Rising into Lawson's Wood, at the western end of **Burton Wood**, the path contours the steep slope through the trees.

LAWSON'S WOOD

The steep, wooded bank overlooking the River Lune is semi-natural woodland, which means that it has developed naturally on undisturbed soils and consequently supports a rich variety of plant life. Although semi-natural the woods have been managed, and the trees were extensively coppiced over centuries for the manufacture of charcoal. More recent management includes removing sycamore, which is not a native tree, and encouraging areas felled during the 1960s to return to their natural state. The predominant species is sessile oak, with ash, elm and small-leaved lime growing in the ravines.

A good time to visit is during spring before the canopy bursts into full leaf, when the understorey is carpeted in wild flowers. Bluebells and ransom create vast sweeps of colour, but primrose, foxglove and wood speedwell are among the many other plants to be found. Such a diverse plant life gives rise to an abundance of insects, which in turn supports a wide range of birds. Pied flycatcher, treecreeper, woodpecker, chiffchaff and several species of tit are among those regularly seen, as well as oystercatcher and sandpiper along the river.

Emerging at the far side of the wood, carry on past a bridge spanning the river. It is part of the 96-mile (155km) pipeline that carries water from Thirlmere to Manchester, and is the longest gravity-fed aqueduct in the country. The path stays beside the river for another mile (1.6km), eventually reaching the railway viaduct at the **Crook o'Lune**. Climb up through the trees back to the car park.

WALK 33
Halton, the Crook o'Lune and Gray's Seat

Start Point	Crook o'Lune SD 521 647
Distance	4 miles (6.4km)
Time	1¾hrs
Terrain	Riverside paths
Height Gain	115m (377ft)
Maps	Explorer OL41 – Forest of Bowland and Ribblesdale
Refreshments	Seasonal café at start and The Greyhound at Halton
Toilets	At start
Parking	Car park at start

Heading up the valley from Lancaster, the first dramatic view along Lunesdale is revealed from a crag above a dramatic U-bend of the river, the Crook o' Lune. The stunning scene inspired Romantic writers and painters such as Gray, Wordsworth, Turner and Cuitt, while early tourist books such as Thomas West's *Guide to the Lakes* ensured its inclusion within a British 'Grand Tour'. Despite two centuries of arboreal growth the view from Gray's Seat can still be appreciated, and is featured in this riverside ramble to nearby Halton.

Riverbank pavilion below Halton Mills

A path paralleling the lane leaves the rear of the overflow car park at the **Crook o'Lune**. Part-way along, pass through a gap onto the road, going briefly right before crossing to a kissing-gate, from which a path drops to the River Lune. Head downstream through woods, breaking to more open ground beyond a footbridge spanning a side-stream. Carry on to a **weir**, where a stepped path descends to a broad, paved quay, below which the river tumbles over a rocky bed, churning the water white.

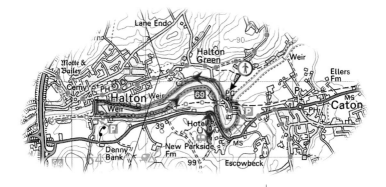

During the 18th century the river was harnessed for **industry**, driving bellows and hammers to forge iron, the furnaces fuelled with charcoal produced in the woods some 2 miles (3.2km) upriver. By the 19th century there was also a mill processing raw cotton imported from the West Indies. The industries declined after the Second World War, and, while few of the buildings remain, the site is being redeveloped for eco-accommodation and workspace.

On reaching buildings that were once part of Halton Mills, there are steps down to a small pavilion and terrace, a viewpoint over the river. Climb back and continue past the abandoned mill buildings, but watch for a path delving into the riverbank trees. Eventually come out at the edge of the development and follow a higher path out left to join a lane into **Halton**. The Greyhound pub is up to the right, but the way back lies to the left over a narrow bridge spanning the river.

Although now a dormitory for Lancaster, **Halton** is an ancient settlement and there is a finely carved Viking cross in the churchyard. It was, together with other manors of Lunesdale, held by Earl Tostig, whose treacherous scheming for his brother's crown brought his untimely end at the Battle of Stamford

Bridge. But King Harold had little chance to savour his victory, for William of Normandy's invasion fleet had already landed. Harold immediately turned his army south, but despite a hard-fought encounter at Hastings, the king was slain and the English defeated. The Normans consolidated their rule with the construction of motte and baileys up and down the country, one being here at Halton overlooking the river.

On the south bank, swing left behind a brick warehouse, part of Halton Station, whose railway platform lies on the other side of the building.

Known affectionately as the **'Little North-Western'**, the railway line ultimately ran between Skipton and Morecambe harbour, the section here opening in 1849. Busy with both passengers and goods, it was extended to the new harbour at Heysham in 1904 and helped make Morecambe one of the north-west's early holiday destinations. The section of line west of Wennington was closed under Beeching's reforms in 1966, but has seen new life as a footpath and cycle track between Morecambe and Caton. The narrow bridge was built to connect Halton with its station, and was originally a toll-bridge.

Go behind the building to find a riverside path through the trees below the embankment, but just beyond a weir, keep an eye open for steps back up to the cycleway. Carry on above the foaming water, later dropping back to a second weir. The path skirts a small compound beside the sluices and then returns to the river. A little further upstream is a takeoff, from which water can be pumped to the River Wyre at Abbeystead to supply other parts of Lancashire.

Continue beside a lovely open stretch of the river before entering a wood. Approaching the first of two railway viaducts spanning the Crook O' Lune, cross a stile and stay by the river to pass beneath its arch. A little

further on, steps take the path up to a junction at the top of the bank. Go right to meet the main road, crossing to the pavement opposite. Follow it briefly right, leaving through a squeeze-stile signed to **Gray's Seat**. A path climbs at the edge of a wood to the viewpoint.

Despite its overgrowth of trees, Gray's Seat is still a pleasing spot to relax

Return to the road and cross back into the wood, but at the junction there now carry on ahead through **Low Mill Wood**. A stepped path shortly descends to the river to wind around the contorted Crook. Emerging from the trees, continue upriver at the edge of open grass. Climb to the road at **Penny Bridge** and cross to a path opposite, which leads to the cycle track. Go left across the eastern viaduct back to the car park.

WALK 34

Slyne and the Lune Aqueduct

Start Point	Riverside Park, Lancaster (off A683 near Skerton Bridge) (SD 481 624)
Distance	6¼ miles (10.1km)
Time	2¾hrs
Terrain	Canal and field paths
Height Gain	110m (360ft)
Maps	Explorer 296 – Lancaster, Morecambe and Fleetwood
Refreshments	The Keys at Slyne
Toilets	In Lancaster
Parking	Car park at start

Designed by John Rennie and completed in 1797, the Lune Aqueduct is one of the great engineering achievements of the Lancaster Canal's construction and carries the waterway high above the River Lune. It is featured in this uncomplicated ramble that follows the canal from Lancaster to the village of Slyne and returns across fields from which there are panoramic views to the city and the Bowland hills.

The towpath and canal on the Lune Aqueduct

Join the riverside Millennium Park path behind the car park and follow it right towards the Lune Aqueduct, passing a **weir** that now defines the tidal limit. Turn off immediately before the aqueduct to find a flight of steps climbing onto the embankment. Follow the towpath across the **aqueduct** and beneath a graceful basket-handle arched road bridge. After swinging behind houses, the canal finally leaves the suburbs to contour across the fields. Follow the canal for almost 2 miles (3.2km) to pass beneath bridge number 115.

Abandon the towpath just beyond the bridge, doubling back to cross the bridge. A hedged track rises away, shortly joining a drive that leads out to Hasty Brow Road. Turn left into **Slyne**, continuing over the crossroads along Throstle Grove. At the end, opposite The Keys, go right onto Lancaster Road.

Beside the junction stand the village stocks and a small walled garden created from the medieval **pinfold**. This was used to impound straying livestock grazing common land whose owners had no rights to the privilege, the animals being released only upon payment of a fine.

Leave after 200m over a stile on the left by a speed limit sign and make for a kissing-gate. Maintaining the same line, climb across the next field to a stile in the top corner. Walk on a short distance and then slip through a gate on the left, cutting the corner to another stile. Head straight across a field, but in the next field strike out to the far-left corner at the top of the hill. Across Morecambe Bay, the Lakeland fells stretch from Black Combe to The Old Man of Coniston and the mountains above Kentmere, while around to the east are the hills of the Yorkshire Dales and Bowland fells.

Stride on by the left boundary, gently losing height. Entering the third field, watch for a waymark directing you left to a stile in the corner, and continue with the hedge now on your right. Walking beneath overhead cables, bear away to the right-hand one of two gates. Follow a stream at the edge of a couple of fields to emerge onto a gravel track beside the **canal**. Go left, but where the track then bends, hop over a stile on the right. Stay by the right boundary, climbing out of the field corner onto the lane by **Halton Bridge**. Cross the bridge and drop to the canal towpath. Go back over the **aqueduct** and retrace your outward route to the car park.

WALK 35

Around Lancaster

Start Point	New Quay Road, Lancaster (SD 464 621)
Distance	6 miles (9.7km)
Time	2½hrs
Terrain	River and canal side-paths, city streets
Height Gain	90m (295ft)
Maps	Explorer 296 – Lancaster, Morecambe and Fleetwood
Refreshments	Pubs and cafés in Lancaster
Toilets	In Lancaster
Parking	Large lay-by at start

River, canal and railway have all contributed to Lancaster's importance over two millennia, and this walk links all three, revealing facets of the town's intriguing history. Beginning along the wharves that sparked Lancaster's growth in the late 17th century, it then winds past historic buildings that act as milestones in its development. The continuing route follows the canal, which opened new trade with Kendal, Preston and beyond and helped sustain Lancaster's status as a port when the river became un-navigable. Joining the riverside branch railway, which superseded the canal link to Glasson Dock, the return finishes above the marshes, where the salt grazing was partly drained during the 18th and 19th centuries for agriculture and to create space for Lancaster's industrial development.

Follow the promenade road towards the city, passing the former factories and warehouses that line **St George's Quay**. Beyond Carlisle Bridge, erected in 1846 for the Lancaster and Carlisle Railway, is the former **Custom House**. It was built in 1764 to a design by Richard Gillow, whose father Robert had founded the famous Gillow furniture company. It is now a Maritime Museum that charts the trading and industrial history of the port.

Walk onto the **Millennium Bridge**. At the junction in the middle, turn right to return to the southern bank and go right again along a cycleway that follows the former

Former quayside warehouses have now been converted into residential apartments

*The main gate of
Lancaster Castle, still
a working prison*

railway to Lancaster's second port at Glasson Dock. After
100m leave left up steps on a path signed to the Roman
Baths, Priory and Castle. Part-way up the hill, detour left
to see the bathhouse, for although little remains standing,
the hypocaust or under-floor heating system is well preserved. Carry on to the church.

THE PRIORY CHURCH AND CASTLE

The priory church and castle dominate the top of the hill, overlying the foundations of a Roman fort built in AD79. The Christian tradition along the Irish Sea coast dates from the first millennium, and a church is known to have stood here in 630. A Benedictine priory was established in 1094 by Roger de Poitou, a Norman nobleman. At one time he held extensive estates throughout England, although he was subsequently exiled for supporting an unsuccessful rebellion against Henry I. After the dissolution in 1539, the priory church continued to be used by the parish.

Roger de Poitou is thought to have founded the castle at about the same time as the monastery as a simple motte and bailey. Curiously, the stone keep may have been built by David I of Scotland, who was awarded the Honour of Lancaster by King Stephen in exchange for his support during the civil war against his cousin Matilda for the crown. From the start, the castle served as a prison and court, functions it still performs almost 1000 years later, although times have changed sufficiently for executions no longer to take place there. Even though it remains a working prison, parts of the castle are open daily for guided tours.

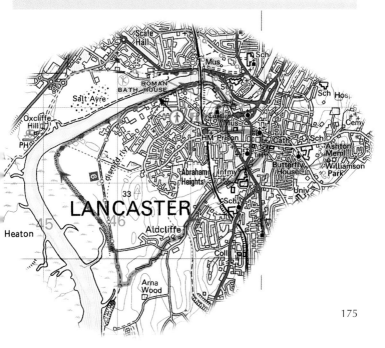

175

Go down between the church and castle to curve right along St Mary's Parade. A short way along, turn sharp left down Castle Hill to the Judges' Lodgings, Lancaster's oldest town house.

> The **Judges' Lodgings** dates from the 16th century and was, for a period, the residence of Thomas Covell, Keeper of the Castle and an enthusiastic witch hunter. It subsequently served to accommodate judges visiting the Assize Courts in the castle, but is now restored as a museum, which in addition to portraying the history of the building has a fine collection of Gillow furniture and a nostalgic assortment of toys.

Head back up Castle Hill and bear left below the castle. At the end go left to the main road, crossing to the pedestrianised Market Street opposite.

> Overlooking Market Square is the **old Town Hall**, which was built in 1783 as the Corn Exchange and now houses the City Museum. The buildings tucked in the corner beside it once served as the town's first telephone exchange, which opened in 1885 with just three subscribers.

Continue through a shopping arcade at the end to emerge on Great John Street. Cross to Friars Passage and then go right into **Dalton Square**.

> Facing the bronze statue of Queen Victoria is the Town Hall, both given to the town by **Lord Ashton**, whose thriving linoleum and coated-fabric business was once Lancaster's major employer. Ashton also built the copper-domed pavilion that rises as a landmark from the centre of Williamson Park as a memorial to his wife.

Go left at the end and walk up Nelson Street, crossing the Lancaster Canal to **St Peter's Catholic Cathedral**.

There turn right and go right again at the next cross-roads. Approaching the canal bridge, drop left to follow the **canal** past the waterfront White Cross and under Penny Bridge.

The waterway runs past former loading basins, the towpath then winding onto the other bank on an elegant roving bridge, which enabled the towing horse to cross without having to disconnect the line. Continue beside Aldcliffe Road and beneath the railway. After a little less than ½ mile (800m), where road and canal part, abandon the towpath, crossing to a lane beside a lodge. It climbs through parkland to **Aldcliffe**, dropping past houses to a junction. A footpath signed to the River Lune leaves through a gate opposite. Behind the houses, wind along a pleasant hedged track, turning right as it enters a field. Near the corner of a second field, cross a stile on the right and walk to the former **railway embankment**.

The way lies to the right, looking out across the salt-marsh to the river. Reaching the end of a lane, leave the ongoing cycle path and cross a stile to the left. Continue on top of the outer flood embankment across Aldcliffe Marsh, where the rising tide floods the channels and the rich mud attracts a profusion of feeding birds. The river bends in front of an early 18th-century smugglers' inn on the opposite bank, the Golden Ball. Often visited by press gangs, the inn became known as 'Snatchems'.

A favourite haunt for press gangs, the Golden Ball across the river became known as 'Snatchems'

Beyond a kissing-gate, leave the main path to stay by the water's edge until the path turns onto the promenade at **New Quay**. Follow the road back to the start. If the final section of the riverside path is flooded, remain with the main path from the kissing-gate past a small light industrial estate to return along the road.

WALK 36
The Lune and the Lancaster Canal

Start Point	Conder Green (SD 456 562)
Distance	6¼ miles (10.1km)
Time	2¾hrs
Terrain	Cycle path, field paths and canal towpath
Height Gain	100m (328ft)
Maps	Explorer 296 – Lancaster, Morecambe and Fleetwood
Refreshments	Café d'Lune and Stork Inn at Conder Green
Toilets	At start
Parking	Car park at start

During the 18th and 19th centuries, Lancaster grew to be one of the busiest trading ports in the country. Originally, ships passed up and down the River Lune on the tide. But, with bigger vessels and silting of the channel, passage became impractical and a dock was ultimately built at Glasson. The cargoes were then transported into Lancaster – in the early days by barge up the river, later along the canal and, after the railway was built, by rail. This walk begins beside the Lune along the trackbed of the old railway, now incorporated within the Millennium Park Cycleway, and returns by way of the Lancaster Canal. The route can be combined with Walk 37 to include the Glasson Branch of the canal.

Head north from the car park at **Conder Green** along the cycle path, overlooking a fringe of marsh and the river.

After some 1¾ miles (2.4km), at a small viewpoint and picnic area, abandon the cycle path for a track signed to Stodday. Beyond the entrance to a **water-treatment plant**, the way becomes a lane. Take the first turning on the right to wind up through **Stodday**. At the top, go right again and later bend left, soon reaching the main road. Follow it left a short distance before leaving along a track on the right. Signed as a footpath to Burrow Road, it leads to a high bridge spanning the canal at Whinney Carr.

The bridge across the canal by Whinney Carr

179

Drop right to the **canal** and follow the towpath away from the bridge. The canal initially runs within a deep wooded cutting, and there is much to look out for along the way. Wild flowers abound in the banks and at the water's edge and there is always plenty of birdlife – you might even spot a kingfisher. Further on, look out too for a siphon, where a stream passes beneath the canal, and for the decaying mechanism of an old sluice gate that allowed a section of the canal to be drained for maintenance.

Eventually, after 1¾ miles (2.4km) and approaching houses on the opposite bank, watch for a stile in the hedge. If combining this route with Walk 37 remain with the towpath; otherwise, to return to Conder Green, enter the field and bear right, passing the end of a clump of trees to join the boundary of a wood. Pass through a gate and walk on into a shallow corner where a stile takes the way into Forerigg Wood. Breaking out on the far side, head straight uphill, aiming left of a pylon. Cresting the rise, a superb view opens ahead across Morecambe Bay. Keeping the same line, drop to a small metal ladder-stile and continue over a second stile. Carry on beside the right-hand hedge over the next low rise, negotiating a stile to continue on its other flank down to **Parkside Farm**.

Walk through the yard and cross a stile in front. Keep on at the edge of a couple of fields to pass Crow Wood. Through a narrow stile there, turn right over a slab bridge and second stile. Follow the hedgerow to the left, continuing past Webster's Farm to emerge onto a junction of lanes. Go right to the main road and then left to the Stork Inn at **Conder Green**, there branching right to return past the Café d'Lune to the car park.

WALK 37

Glasson Dock and the Lancaster Canal Spur

Start Point	Conder Green (SD 456 562)
Distance	6 miles (9.7km)
Time	2½hrs
Terrain	Field paths and canal towpath
Height Gain	60m (197ft)
Maps	Explorer 296 – Lancaster, Morecambe and Fleetwood
Refreshments	Pubs and cafés at Conder Green, Galgate Marina, Thurnham and Glasson Dock
Toilets	At start and Glasson Dock
Parking	Car park at start

Although some cargo is still shipped through Glasson Dock, it is now used mainly by leisure craft, which arrive here both from the sea and by travelling inland along the canal. The dock is included in this pleasant countryside walk from Conder Green, which takes in both the Lancaster Canal and the spur that subsequently connected the dock to Lancaster.

GLASSON DOCK

Towards the end of the 18th century, Lancaster's role as a major port was threatened as it became impossible to keep the main channel sufficiently clear of silt for the passage of seagoing ships. Some already moored and often unloaded cargoes for transhipment at Sunderland, on the far bank of the Lune, but in 1779 it was decided to build a dock at Glasson.

After initial difficulties the new dock, capable of holding 25 ships, was completed in 1787. Cargoes were offloaded onto barges and taken upriver, but the construction of the Lancaster Canal offered a better option. The canal branch to Glasson Dock eventually opened in 1825, dropping from a junction just south of Galgate through six locks to reach sea level. A freshwater basin and lock connected the canal with the harbour dock, and smaller seagoing craft could pass directly into the canal system at high tide.

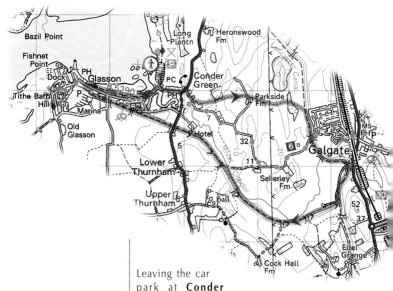

Leaving the car park at **Conder Green**, walk back to the junction by the Stork Inn. Go left and immediately sharp right. At the next junction, cross a stile on the left and head upfield past Webster's Farm. At the top corner, hop over a stile on the right, cross a slab bridge and then turn left through a second stile. Carry on at the field edge to **Parkside Farm**.

Keep ahead between the barns and through a field gate at the far side, climbing away by the right-hand boundary. At the top, cross to the opposite flank of the hedge and continue into a dip. Negotiate a couple of stiles and carry on over a rising pasture, dropping beyond into Forerigg Wood. Emerging over a stile, go right at the field edge. Beyond a gate, keep the same straight line past a clump of trees to reach the **canal** towpath.

Follow the canal to the right, shortly passing **Galgate Marina**, where you can detour over the bridge to the pub. The onward route, however, sticks with the towpath, which soon leads to a junction with the **Glasson Branch**.

Leaving the main canal, follow the spur down past a succession of locks. Although only of modest length, this walk is amply blessed with refreshment stops, and there is yet another pub at **Thurnham** in what used to be a mill. The canal continues for almost another mile to **Glasson**.

A canal boat passes beneath Ellel Hall Bridge by Galgate Marina

A motley collection of craft now moor at Glasson

Leave the canal at the foot of the **marina**, crossing the car park to find a path leaving on the opposite side of the road between a public convenience and The Victoria Inn. Climbing onto the sea wall, the route follows the former course of the Glasson railway out of the village, later crossing the River Conder to return you to the car park at **Conder Green**.

WALK 38
Cockersand Abbey

Start Point	Glasson Dock marina (SD 445 560)
Distance	7 miles (11.3km)
Time	3hrs
Terrain	Field paths and lanes
Height Gain	70m (230ft)
Maps	Explorer 296 – Lancaster, Morecambe and Fleetwood
Refreshments	Glasson
Toilets	Glasson
Parking	Car park at start

Much of the coastal farmland surrounding the Lune estuary has been claimed from the tidal marshes, its flatness broken by occasional low hills that offer surprisingly expansive views. This undemanding walk from Glasson angles around the deep ditches that drain the countryside and, like hedges, provide habitats for birds and other wildlife. After cresting the highest of the hills at Norbreck, the ramble returns along the coastal dyke, passing Cockersand Abbey and the Plover Scar lighthouse.

Follow the road across the lock at the foot of **Glasson Dock marina**, climbing beyond to a junction at the top of **Tithe Barn Hill**, a superb viewpoint overlooking the marshes at the mouth of the River Lune. Go left down the hill and, at the next junction, keep ahead along Dobbs

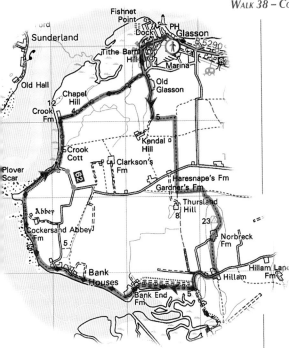

Lane. Some ¼ mile (400m) beyond **Old Glasson Farm**, and approaching a cattle-grid at the entrance to **Kendal Hill Farm**, leave through a gate on the left. About 20m before the end of the grass track, take the gate into the right-hand field and walk its length to find a stile beyond an indented corner. Carry on to emerge behind a wooden hut onto **Moss Lane**.

Diagonally opposite, a waymark indicates a foot-bridge into another field. Walk away by the fence to the bottom corner and cross a stile on the left. Head out by a reed-filled ditch at the foot of successive fields to a stile, part-way along the fourth field. Follow the fence towards a low hill, going through a gate on the left when the way

185

Only the chapter house remains from Cockersand Abbey

is barred by a drain. Skirt around its head and climb the **hill**, there joining a track that winds around a small pond.

The mound, like the others erupting from the coastal plain, is a **drumlin**, a glacial feature formed by deposition and erosion at the edge of a retreating ice sheet. Although only 23m above sea level, the trig column commands a panorama that would do credit to many a mountain summit.

Follow the track down to **Norbreck Farm**. Swing right in front of the old farmhouse, but then leave left over a stile beside a cattle-grid at the entrance to a new house. Hop over a second stile on the right and head downhill across the fields to **Hillam Farm**. Walk through the yard and past the farmhouse onto Hillam Lane.

To the right, the lane winds towards the coast, dropping through a flood dyke onto the edge of the marsh. Turn right and walk to **Bank End Farm**, passing around it along a path above the sands. Stay with the coast beyond the next farm, **Bank Houses**, where there is the ruin of a wartime lookout. Rising onto the embankment, the path leads to the ruin of **Cockersand Abbey**.

COCKERSAND ABBEY

During the 12th century, this corner of Lancashire was a wild and lonely place, an almost featureless expanse of tidal marsh. Yet, it was just such spots that attracted religious devouts, who shunned the materialistic world in search of spirituality and lived as hermits, often serving the poor and sick. One such man was Hugh Garth, who established a cell here in 1180. His reputation grew, and within 10 years the priory of St Mary of the Marsh was founded under the Premonstratensian order. It grew to an abbey and became one of the richest religious houses in Lancashire.

Abandoned after the Dissolution the abbey quickly became a ruin, and the stone of its once beautiful buildings was plundered for the neighbouring farms and the wall that now keeps the tide at bay. Only the chapter house remains, an enigmatic reminder of the abbey's glorious past, preserved by the Daltons, who subsequently acquired the estate, as the family burial vault.

Continue around the point of Plover Hill, off which stands the **Plover Scar Light**. It was built in 1847 and marks the mouth of the Lune, although the channel runs west for another 4 miles (6.4km) between tide-washed sandbanks before finally becoming lost in the sea.

The Plover Scar Light marks the edge of the channel

The path joins a track past a small parking area to meet the corner of a lane beside Lighthouse Cottage, which stands on the site of the original abbey lighthouse. The coastal lane leads on to **Crook Farm**, where the route finally turns inland in front of the farmhouse along a hedged track. Becoming less distinct, it crosses the head of a creek and later rises to a small caravan park. From there, follow the metalled lane to the junction at **Dobbs Lane** and go left back to Glasson Dock. Approaching the **marina** lock, look across to the far corner of the lower basin. The curious small building dwarfed by the modern storage sheds is the old Glasson Lighthouse, which is said to be the smallest in England.

WALK 39

Overton and Bazil Point

Start Point	Overton (SD 436 580)
Distance	2¾ miles (4.4km)
Time	1¼hrs
Terrain	Lane, field and coastal paths
Height Gain	60m (197ft)
Maps	Explorer 296 – Lancaster, Morecambe and Fleetwood
Refreshments	Pubs in Overton
Toilets	None
Parking	Roadside parking in Overton
Note	The shore path around Bazil Point can be flooded at high tide.

Overton straddles a spur of high ground overlooking the Lune's estuary, almost an island surrounded by drained marshes and the river. During the 19th century the village benefited from the increasing tourist trade brought to the Lancashire coast by the railways, and it was a popular excursion from the nearby resorts of Morecambe and Heysham. Its ancient church and Bazil Point are included in this short ramble, which ends by climbing the village's modest hill for a surprisingly stunning panoramic view.

In **Overton** follow a sign to the church, then leave the crossroads in the village centre along Chapel Lane, which eventually swings sharply left to St Helen's Church.

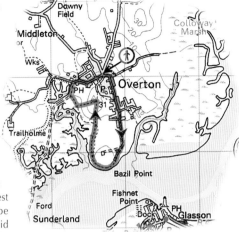

> **St Helen's Church** was once a chapel under St Mary's at Lancaster and is claimed to be one of the oldest churches in Lancashire. The thick west wall is considered to be Saxon, while the splendid carving surrounding the doorway is a fine example of early 12th-century Norman work. The over-large northern transept, however, was added in the 19th century to accommodate an increasing congregation as the village expanded.

Return to the sharp bend and now go left along Bazil Lane, signed to Sunderland Point Road. Becoming a track, it runs across a field beyond the houses. On approaching a cattle-grid at the far side, bear left to a kissing-gate, from which a path leads to the flood embankment. Cross onto the foreshore and turn right.

Beyond Ferry Cottage, once the home of the ferryman who plied between here and Glasson on the far bank, walk at the head of the shingle beach around **Bazil Point**. Where the ground underfoot returns to grass look for a stile, over which you can continue along the embankment. Later rejoin the shore and immediately cross a second stile to the right. Climb away by the right hedge to a stile in the corner and carry on up the field to a **trig column** on top of the hill. At 31m high it is by no means the lowest survey column in the land, but even

189

Low tide exposes banks of mud beyond the salt marsh off Bazil Point

this modest height gives a far-reaching view along the Lancashire coast. However, it is not quite high enough to spot the Isle of Man, which lies some 65 miles (105km) to the west.

Leave the summit left, dropping to a prodigious stile onto the edge of the marsh. Turn right to reach a lane, a tide-washed highway that leads out to Sunderland. To the right, however, it leads back into **Overton**, passing the village's two pubs – both of their names reflecting maritime connections.

The Romans established a settlement on the high ground of **Overton**, probably a signal station to give warning of unwelcome visitors to the garrison at Lancaster. Overlooking tidal creeks and surrounded by rich pasture, it later prospered as a fishing and farming community, and for over 300 years boasted a boat-building yard. The village also provided pilots, who used their intimate knowledge of the estuary's currents and hidden sandbanks to navigate sea-going vessels up and down the river to the port at Lancaster.

WALK 40

Sunderland Point

Start Point	Potts Corner, Middleton (SD 412 572)
Distance	4½ miles (7.2km)
Time	2hrs
Terrain	Field and coast paths
Height Gain	30m (98ft)
Maps	Explorer 296 – Lancaster, Morecambe and Fleetwood
Refreshments	None
Toilets	None
Parking	Car park at start

The River Lune enters Morecambe Bay and the Irish Sea beyond the tip of Sunderland Point, although at low tide the channel now runs on the southern side of the estuary past the light marking the gravel bank of Plover Scar. This circuit around the low-lying peninsula takes in the tiny village of Sunderland, which developed during the early 18th century as a staging port for Lancaster.

From **Potts Corner** walk back along the lane for ½ mile (800m) before turning off right on a track marked as a footpath to Middleton.

> **Middleton Holiday Camp**, which lay just to the north, opened in 1939 and became, literally, the flagship of the Pontin empire – the entertainment complex, around which its chalets clustered, was a recreation of the famous Cunard luxury liner the SS Berengaria. But despite the popularity of all-in 'Hi-de-Hi' holiday-camp entertainment, the Lancashire coast could not compete with Spanish sunshine or the lure of cheap continental package holidays, and the camp finally closed in 1993.

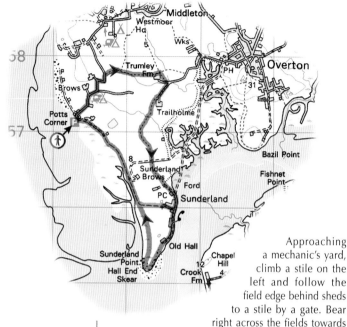

Approaching a mechanic's yard, climb a stile on the left and follow the field edge behind sheds to a stile by a gate. Bear right across the fields towards **Trumley Farm**, bypassing it on the left and ultimately emerging through a kissing-gate onto a track, Trailholme Road.

Go right, leaving on the bend over a stile. Walk beside the farm to join another track and take the right branch where it forks. After 20m, the signed footpath slips through the hedge onto the adjacent track, recrossing it a short distance further on to skirt **Trailholme Farm**. Climbing an embankment, pass through a gate; however, just before a second gate, drop left to a ladder-stile. Go right into a large pasture and make for a stile near the far-right corner. Walk left to a footbridge and amble on towards Sunderland's buildings. More bridges span intervening ditches and, after the third, bear left to the far corner. Climb over the embankment onto the foreshore and turn right through the hamlet of **Sunderland**.

Sunderland's filial-topped gatepost is as famous as the 'cotton tree' that used to grow here

SUNDERLAND

Despite its road being swamped twice a day by the tide and 'sundering' it from the mainland, Sunderland grew during the 18th century as a busy port. Warehouses lined the quay to store goods awaiting transhipment to Lancaster, and a blacksmith, ropery and blockmaker's shop refitted ships for their next voyage. The entrepreneur behind Sunderland's development was a Quaker merchant, Robert Lawson, whose business included the African slave trade. However, he appears to have overstretched himself, for by 1773 he was bankrupt.

In spite of this trade continued, and vessels left Britain with manufactured goods to be traded along the African coast for slaves. They were shipped across the Atlantic to labour on the West Indies' plantations, while the ships returned with cargoes of cotton, timber, tobacco and molasses. The port declined towards the end of the century as the channel silted, and ships berthed instead at Glasson's new dock across the river.

During the early part of the 19th century, Sunderland enjoyed a brief revival as a resort offering sea baths, first within a small indoor pool and then, as patrons became more daring, from bathing machines into the sea itself.

At the filial-topped gate pillar, a bridleway known as The Lane cuts across the headland and provides an easy short-cut when the foreshore around the point is flooded during exceptional tides. Otherwise, carry on past cottages, some of which have been converted from Lawson's 18th-century warehouses. After the last of the cottages the way drops to the head of the shore beneath low crumbling cliffs of clay. Across the mouth of the Lune is the Plover Scar Light, behind which a low building is the chapter house of Cockersand Abbey. Rounding the point, the view is then to the north, the massive, squat buildings in the middle distance being the nuclear power station at Heysham.

Through a gate, the path runs behind extensive salt marshes, shortly passing **Sambo's Grave**, which lies in a small enclosure on the right. Just beyond, The Lane comes across from the village of Sunderland. Keep ahead along a rough track at the tide line, which leads back to **Potts Corner**.

Taken from Africa to the West Indies as a child slave, **Sambo** arrived in Sunderland around 1736. He was servant to the captain of a trading ship and was left here while his master went upriver to conduct business in Lancaster. Either pining because he thought he had been abandoned or succumbing to illness, the lad died before the captain returned and was buried in an unmarked grave. The memorial, still tended by local schoolchildren, was placed over the grave in 1795 by the Revd James Watson.

Potts Corner looks out across Morecambe Bay to the Furness peninsula and Black Combe

APPENDIX A

Route summary table

Walk	Title	Start	Grid ref	Distance (miles/kms)	Time (hrs)	Height gain (m/ft)	OS Map	Page
1	Weasdale and Randygill Top	Wath	NY 685 050	8/12.9	4¼	560/1837	OL19	29
2	Newbiggin-on-Lune	Ravenstonedale	NY 722 042	6½/10.5	3	240/787	OL19	34
3	Wath to Kelleth	Wath	NY 684 049	4/6.4	1¾	105/344	OL19	40
4	Bowderdale and The Calf	Bowderdale	NY 678 046	11/17.7	5½	605/1985	OL19	43
5	Gaisgill to Orton	Gaisgill	NY 640 053	6½/10.5	3	165/541	OL19	48
6	Orton Scar	Orton	NY 622 082	7/11.3	3¼	270/886	OL19	53
7	Birk Beck	Greenholme	NY 597 057	5½/8.9	2½	175/574	OL7	57
8	Bretherdale	Greenholme	NY 597 057	5/8	2½	225/738	OL7	60
9	Blease Fell	Mount Pleasant, Tebay	NY 618 045	6/9.7	3	325/1066	OL19	64
10	Jeffrey's Mount and Borrowdale	Lune's Bridge, S of Tebay	NY 613 028	7¾/12.5	4	530/1739	OL7 & OL19	69
11	Whinfell and Borrowdale	Near Huck's Bridge, on A6	NY 552 038	9/14.5	4¾	680/2231	OL7	73
12	Carlin Gill	Carlingill Bridge	SD 626 996	3¼/5.2	1½	245/804	OL19	78
13	Beck Foot	Beck Foot	SD 616 965	5/8	2½	280/918	OL19	81

Walk	Title	Start	Grid ref	Distance (miles/ kms)	Time (hrs)	Height gain (m/ft)	OS Map	Page
14	Firbank and Bridge End	Goodies, on B6257	SD 625 943	5/8	2½	290/951	OL19	85
15	Winder, Calders and The Calf	Sedbergh	SD 657 921	9¾/15.7	4½	855/2805	OL19	90
16	Sedbergh and the River Rawthey	Sedbergh	SD 657 921	5/8	2¼	145/477	OL19	95
17	Frostrow Fells and Dentdale	Sedbergh	SD 656 920	6¾/10.9	3¼	295/962	OL2 & OL19	100
18	Beside the River Dee from Dent	Dent	SD 704 871	6/9.7	2½	130/427	OL2	104
19	Killington	Killington New Bridge	SD 622 908	6½/10.5	3	280/919	OL2 & OL19	107
20	Calf Top	Barbon	SD 628 823	8¼/13.3	5¼	665/2182	OL2	112
21	Barbon Low Fell	Barbon	SD 628 823	8½/13.7	4¼	420/1378	OL2	116
22	Around Casterton	Devil's Bridge, Kirkby Lonsdale	SD 616 782	5¼/8.4	2½	160/525	OL2	120
23	Kirkby Lonsdale	Devil's Bridge, Kirkby Lonsdale	SD 616 782	6½/10.5	3	160/525	OL2	124
24	By the Lune from Kirkby Lonsdale	Devil's Bridge, Kirkby Lonsdale	SD 616 782	5¼/8.4	2½	130/427	OL2	128
25	Leck Beck	Cowan Bridge	SD 635 764	8½/13.7	3½	360/1181	OL2	133
26	Arkholme and the River Lune	Arkholme	SD 584 721	6¾/10.9	3	180/591	OL2 & OL7	137

Walk	Title	Start	Grid ref	Distance (miles/kms)	Time (hrs)	Height gain (m/ft)	OS Map	Page
27	Melling	Loyn Bridge	SD 580 697	5½/8.8	2½	145/476	OL2	141
28	Roeburndale	Barkin Bridge	SD 600 638	8/12.9	4	442/1450	OL41	145
29	Whit Moor	Claughton Quarry	SD 570 643	6¼/10.1	3	300/984	OL41	150
30	Littledale	Rigg Lane, Quernmore	SD 526 604	8¼/13.3	4	385/1263	OL41	154
31	Clougha Pike	Rigg Lane, Quernmore	SD 526 604	5½/8.8	2¾	365/1197	OL41	158
32	Aughton and the River Lune	Crook o'Lune	SD 521 647	7¼/11.7	3¼	195/640	OL41	161
33	Halton, the Crook o'Lune and Gray's Seat	Crook o'Lune	SD 521 647	4/6.4	1¾	115/377	OL41	165
34	Slyne and the Lune Aqueduct	Riverside Park, Lancaster	SD 481 624	6¼/10.1	2¾	110/360	296	170
35	Around Lancaster	New Quay Road, Lancaster	SD 464 621	6/9.7	2½	90/295	296	172
36	The Lune and the Lancaster Canal	Conder Green	SD 456 562	6¼/10.1	2¾	100/328	296	178
37	Glasson Dock and the Lancaster Canal Spur	Conder Green	SD 456 562	6/9.7	2½	60/197	296	181
38	Cockersand Abbey	Glasson Dock marina	SD 445 560	7/11.3	3	70/230	296	184
39	Overton and Bazil Point	Overton	SD 436 580	2¾/4.4	1¼	60/197	296	188
40	Sunderland Point	Potts Corner, Middleton	SD 412 572	4½/7.2	2	30/98	296	191

A linear walk along the Lune Valley presents an enticing prospect. At some 60 miles (96km), and with no daunting wilderness sections to negotiate, it offers a comfortable five- or six-day challenge for any reasonably fit countryside walker, while those yearning for something more demanding will find abundant distractions in the neighbouring hills and many side-valleys. The logistics are uncomplicated, too, with local buses serving both Newbiggin-on-Lune and Glasson Dock, and convenient overnight accommodation at the main towns and villages along the way.

The absence of a waymark-defined 'Lune Way' adds a dimension of choice to route planning and encourages a more personal exploration. Unfortunately, riverside access is not complete throughout the Lune's length, but there are many sections where a path follows the riverbank or is not too far away. Elsewhere, tracks and paths rise onto neighbouring hills and give wider views across the countryside. Inevitably there is lane walking, but the lanes are quiet and their flower-rich hedgerows make them a delight to follow. For those comfortable with map and compass,

Looking down Dale Gill from the source of the Lune

navigation should not present a problem, although paths across the bordering moorland uplands can be faint and are not recommended for novice walkers when visibility is poor. Footpaths are generally signed from the point at which they leave a lane, but subsequent waymarking is not always comprehensive and attention to the map is necessary.

Planning an intended route can be almost as enjoyable as following it on the ground, as you contemplate which places to include or choose between alternative paths to gain the best prospect for a view. One of the main considerations is determining which side of the river to be on for any given stretch. A cursory glance at the map suggests an abundance of crossing points, but several are simply fords, particularly those used by bridleways. Note, too, that a couple of bridges – that on the Underley estate and the Haweswater Aqueduct, to the north and south of Kirkby Lonsdale respectively – have no pedestrian right of access. Motorway and railway bridges are similarly unhelpful to the walker, although the experience of crossing the Lancaster Canal's aqueduct, just east of the city, is something not to be missed, even if only by way of detour.

Perhaps the first consideration is whether to walk upstream or downstream, for each has merit. Beginning at the river mouth, the route leads progressively towards wilder countryside, although an early detour into the Forest of Bowland AONB emphasises that unbounded moorland overlooks even the final phase of the river before it escapes to the sea. The walker backpacking for the first time might favour this upriver approach as, being closer to 'civilisation' in its early stages, there are more options available should an early abort or change of plan become necessary. Some, however, might take the view that going with the flow brings a greater affinity with the natural order, and that walking from source to sea better reveals the progressive development of the river. There is no right answer; the practicalities of accommodation and transport support both options, the views in either direction are equally magnificent and there are satisfying objectives at either end.

SUGGESTED ITINERARY

An outline itinerary upon which to base a route might be as follows.

Day 1 – Newbiggin-on-Lune
An exploration of the northern Howgills and locating the Lune's two sources beneath Green Bell and at St Helen's Well.

Day 2 – Newbiggin-on-Lune to Tebay (around 6 miles/9.7km)
Follow the lane above the northern bank to Wath, crossing to continue on footpaths to Tebay. This short day would allow a little time to wander into the Howgill dales, to Orton or Greenholme.

The summit of Calf Top

Day 3 – Tebay to Sedbergh
(around 12 miles/19.3km)

A little ingenuity avoids the A685 by taking the western bank via Roundthwaite, then reverting to the eastern bank over the road bridge to follow track and lane beneath the shadow of the Howgills. Join the Dales Way at Crook of Lune Bridge and follow it to Sedbergh, perhaps cutting the corner beneath Winder.

An exciting alternative for experienced walkers confident in navigation is to pick a high-level route across the Howgill tops. One possibility is to follow the ridge onto Blease Fell and then cut across over Uldale Head, dropping beyond into Blakethwaite Bottom before climbing onto Docker Knott. Picking up the National Park boundary, climb on over Bush Howe, eventually gaining the summit of The Calf. With the hard work then behind you, the final leg is a long, undulating descent over Calders, Arant Haw and Winder to Sedbergh.

Day 4 – Sedbergh to Kirkby Lonsdale
(around 15 miles/24.1km)

For a day's moderate walking, largely along quiet lanes, accompany the River Rawthey from Sedbergh and cross the Lune with the B6256. Follow minor lanes down to the bridge at Rigmaden, there crossing to reach Barbon. There are then several options past Casterton to reach the Devil's Bridge in Kirkby Lonsdale. As an alternative, there is a splendid high-level path over Middleton Fell above Dentdale and Barbondale.

Day 5 – Kirkby Lonsdale to Lancaster
(around 16 miles/25.7km)

It can be riverside walking all the way to Lancaster. Start the day on the

The beach below Cockersand Abbey

western bank, crossing at the Crook o'Lune to then follow the Millennium Park Cycleway into the heart of the city.

Day 6 – Lancaster to the Plover Scar Light (around 8 miles/12.9km)
Leave Lancaster on the south bank along St George's Quay and New Quay, eventually picking up a riverside path. Later it joins with the cycleway and continues all the way to Glasson. After a short stretch on the lane over Tithe Barn Hill, a path heads back to the coast and leads past the Plover Scar Light and the ruin of Cockersand Abbey.

As with any undertaking it is a good idea to arrange accommodation in advance, particularly during holiday periods, and, of course, check times of local transport.

APPENDIX C
Useful contacts

National Parks and AONBs
Forest of Bowland AONB
Tel 01200 448000
www.forestofbowland.com

Lake District National Park
Tel 01539 724555
www.lakedistrict.gov.uk

Yorkshire Dales National Park
Tel 0300 456 0030
www.yorkshiredales.org.uk

Tourist Information Centres
Kirkby Lonsdale: Tel 015242 71437
Lancaster: Tel 01524 582394
Sedbergh: Tel 015396 20125

**Rights of Way issues
(outside National Parks)**
Cumbria County Council
Tel 01228 226758
www.cumbria.gov.uk

Lancashire County Council
Tel 01772 534709
www.lancashire.gov.uk

North Yorkshire County Council
Tel 0845 034 9599
www.northyorks.gov.uk

Public transport
Traveline
Tel 0871 200 2233
www.traveline.org.uk

Accommodation
Cumbria
www.visitcumbria.com

Lancashire
Tel 01524 582393
www.visitlancashire.com

Yorkshire
www.yorkshire.com

Camping and Caravanning Club
Tel 024 7647 5448
www.campingandcaravanningclub.co.uk

LISTING OF CICERONE GUIDES

Rocky Rambler's Wild Walks
Scrambles in the Lake District
   North & South
Short Walks in Lakeland
   1 South Lakeland
   2 North Lakeland
   3 West Lakeland
The Cumbria Coastal Way
The Cumbria Way and the
   Allerdale Ramble
Tour of the Lake District

**DERBYSHIRE, PEAK
DISTRICT AND MIDLANDS**
High Peak Walks
Scrambles in the Dark Peak
The Star Family Walks
Walking in Derbyshire
White Peak Walks
   The Northern Dales
   The Southern Dales

SOUTHERN ENGLAND
A Walker's Guide to the
   Isle of Wight
London – The definitive
   walking guide
Suffolk Coast and
   Heaths Walks
The Cotswold Way
The North Downs Way
The South Downs Way
The South West Coast Path
The Thames Path
Walking in Berkshire
Walking in Kent
Walking in Sussex
Walking in the Isles of Scilly
Walking in the
   Thames Valley
Walking on Dartmoor
Walking on Guernsey
Walking on Jersey
Walks in the South Downs
   National Park

**WALES AND WELSH
BORDERS**
Backpacker's Britain – Wales
Glyndwr's Way
Great Mountain Days
   in Snowdonia
Hillwalking in Snowdonia

Hillwalking in Wales
   Vols 1 & 2
Offa's Dyke Path
Ridges of Snowdonia
Scrambles in Snowdonia
The Ascent of Snowdon
The Lleyn Peninsula
   Coastal Path
The Pembrokeshire
   Coastal Path
The Shropshire Hills
The Wye Valley Walk
Walking in Pembrokeshire
Walking on the
   Brecon Beacons
Welsh Winter Climbs

**INTERNATIONAL
CHALLENGES, COLLECTIONS
AND ACTIVITIES**
Canyoning
Europe's High Points
The Via Francigena
   (Canterbury to Rome):
   Part 1

EUROPEAN CYCLING
Cycle Touring in France
Cycle Touring in Ireland
Cycle Touring in Spain
Cycle Touring in Switzerland
Cycling in the French Alps
Cycling the Canal du Midi
Cycling the River Loire
The Danube Cycleway
The Grand Traverse of the
   Massif Central
The Way of St James

AFRICA
Climbing in the
   Moroccan Anti-Atlas
Kilimanjaro: A Complete
   Trekker's Guide
Mountaineering in the
   Moroccan High Atlas
Trekking in the
   Atlas Mountains
Walking in the Drakensberg

**ALPS – CROSS-BORDER
ROUTES**
100 Hut Walks in the Alps

Across the Eastern Alps: E5
Alpine Points of View
Alpine Ski Mountaineering
   1 Western Alps
   2 Central and Eastern Alps
Chamonix to Zermatt
Snowshoeing
Tour of Mont Blanc
Tour of Monte Rosa
Tour of the Matterhorn
Trekking in the Alps
Walking in the Alps
Walks and Treks in the
   Maritime Alps

**PYRENEES AND FRANCE/
SPAIN CROSS-BORDER
ROUTES**
Rock Climbs in The Pyrenees
The GR10 Trail
The Mountains of Andorra
The Pyrenean Haute Route
The Pyrenees
The Way of St James
   France & Spain
Through the Spanish
   Pyrenees: GR11
Walks and Climbs in
   the Pyrenees

AUSTRIA
The Adlerweg
Trekking in Austria's
   Hohe Tauern
Trekking in the Stubai Alps
Trekking in the Zillertal Alps
Walking in Austria

EASTERN EUROPE
The High Tatras
The Mountains of Romania
Walking in Bulgaria's
   National Parks
Walking in Hungary

FRANCE
Ecrins National Park
GR20: Corsica
Mont Blanc Walks
Mountain Adventures in
   the Maurienne
The Cathar Way
The GR5 Trail

The Robert Louis
 Stevenson Trail
Tour of the Oisans: The GR54
Tour of the Queyras
Tour of the Vanoise
Trekking in the Vosges and Jura
Vanoise Ski Touring
Walking in Provence
Walking in the Cathar Region
Walking in the Cevennes
Walking in the Dordogne
Walking in the Haute Savoie
 North & South
Walking in the Languedoc
Walking in the Tarentaise and
 Beaufortain Alps
Walking on Corsica

GERMANY
Germany's Romantic Road
Walking in the Bavarian Alps
Walking in the Harz Mountains
Walking the River Rhine Trail

HIMALAYA
Annapurna: A Trekker's Guide
Bhutan
Everest: A Trekker's Guide
Garhwal and Kumaon:
 A Trekker's and
 Visitor's Guide
Kangchenjunga:
 A Trekker's Guide
Langtang with Gosainkund and
 Helambu: A Trekker's Guide
Manaslu: A Trekker's Guide
The Mount Kailash Trek

IRELAND
Irish Coastal Walks
The Irish Coast to Coast Walk
The Mountains of Ireland

ITALY
Gran Paradiso
Italy's Sibillini National Park
Shorter Walks in the Dolomites
Through the Italian Alps
Trekking in the Apennines
Trekking in the Dolomites
Via Ferratas of the Italian
 Dolomites: Vols 1 & 2
Walking in Abruzzo

Walking in Sardinia
Walking in Sicily
Walking in the Central
 Italian Alps
Walking in the Dolomites
Walking in Tuscany
Walking on the Amalfi Coast

MEDITERRANEAN
Jordan – Walks, Treks, Caves,
 Climbs and Canyons
The Ala Dag
The High Mountains of Crete
The Mountains of Greece
Treks and Climbs in
 Wadi Rum, Jordan
Walking in Malta
Western Crete

NORTH AMERICA
British Columbia
The Grand Canyon
The John Muir Trail
The Pacific Crest Trail

SOUTH AMERICA
Aconcagua and the
 Southern Andes
Hiking and Biking Peru's
 Inca Trails
Torres del Paine

SCANDINAVIA
Trekking in Greenland
Walking in Norway

SLOVENIA, CROATIA AND
MONTENEGRO
The Julian Alps of Slovenia
The Mountains of Montenegro
Trekking in Slovenia
Walking in Croatia

SPAIN AND PORTUGAL
Costa Blanca Walks
 1 West & 2 East
Mountain Walking in
 Southern Catalunya
The Mountains of Central Spain
Trekking through Mallorca
Walking in Madeira
Walking in Mallorca
Walking in the Algarve

Walking in the Canary Islands
 2 East
Walking in the Cordillera
 Cantabrica
Walking in the Sierra Nevada
Walking in La Gomera and
 El Hierro
Walking on La Palma
Walking on Tenerife
Walking the GR7 in Andalucia
Walks and Climbs in the
 Picos de Europa

SWITZERLAND
Alpine Pass Route
Central Switzerland
The Bernese Alps
The Swiss Alps
Tour of the Jungfrau Region
Walking in the Valais
Walking in Ticino
Walks in the Engadine

TECHNIQUES
Geocaching in the UK
Indoor Climbing
Lightweight Camping
Map and Compass
Mountain Weather
Moveable Feasts
Outdoor Photography
Rock Climbing
Sport Climbing
The Book of the Bivvy
The Hillwalker's Guide
 to Mountaineering
The Hillwalker's Manual

MINI GUIDES
Avalanche!
Navigating with a GPS
Navigation
Pocket First Aid and
 Wilderness Medicine
Snow

For full information on all
our guides, and to order
books and eBooks, visit our
website:
www.cicerone.co.uk.

Walking – Trekking – Mountaineering – Climbing – Cycling

Over 40 years, Cicerone have built up an outstanding collection of 300 guides, inspiring all sorts of amazing adventures.

Every guide comes from extensive exploration and research by our expert authors, all with a passion for their subjects. They are frequently praised, endorsed and used by clubs, instructors and outdoor organisations.

All our titles can now be bought as **e-books** and many as iPad and Kindle files and we will continue to make all our guides available for these and many other devices.

Our website shows any **new information** we've received since a book was published. Please do let us know if you find anything has changed, so that we can pass on the latest details. On our **website** you'll also find some great ideas and lots of information, including sample chapters, contents lists, reviews, articles and a photo gallery.

It's easy to keep in touch with what's going on at Cicerone, by getting our monthly **free e-newsletter**, which is full of offers, competitions, up-to-date information and topical articles. You can subscribe on our home page and also follow us on **Facebook** and **Twitter**, as well as our **blog**.

Cicerone – the very best guides for exploring the world.

CICERONE

2 Police Square Milnthorpe Cumbria LA7 7PY
Tel: 015395 62069 info@cicerone.co.uk
www.cicerone.co.uk